DESIGN AND TECHNOLOGY

Resistant materials

JOHN DAVIES • ALAN GOODIER

SERIES EDITORS: PETER BRANSON • 23` 80 577307 OON-SMITH

CAMBRIDGE UNIVERSITY PRESS

Published by the Press Syndicate of the University of Cambridge
The Pitt Building, Trumpington Street, Cambridge CB2 1RP
40 West 20th Street, New York, NY 10011–4211, USA
10 Stamford Road, Oakleigh, Melbourne 3166, Australia

First published 1996

Produced by Gecko Limited, Bicester, Oxon.

Printed in Great Britain at the University Press, Cambridge

A catalogue record for this book is available from the British Library

ISBN 0 521 49873 2

Cover – CDS.

Cover design by Ralf Zeigermann

Acknowledgements
The authors and publisher would like to thank the following
for their help in the preparation of this book.
Caryl Jackamann, Mike Martindell and all the staff at Arcam;
Roger Carr, Phil Kett and all the staff at FM Design;
Glaxo Wellcome plc;
Mike Moore and all the staff at Naim Audio;
Peter Smalley and all the staff at Racal Transcom;
Mr and Mrs Stokes;
Margaret Turner and all her staff;
Colin Watson, Brian Wilson and all the staff at President
Office Furniture;
Rob Davies, Sheila Rockingham and all the staff at Wicksteed
Leisure Limited.

The publisher would like to thank the following for
permission to reproduce copyright material.
British Standards Institute, 15, 20, 21,100;
Loctite UK, 131–134;
MFI International, 107;
Diagrams on page 126 reproduced with permission from
PSM International;
Racal Transcom, 61;
Diagram on page 11 reproduced with permission from HS
Walsh and Son Ltd.

The publisher would like to thank the following for
permission to reproduce copyright photographs.
British Architectural Library, RIBA, London, 18tl;
Carson Office Furniture Systems, 72bl;
John Davies, 7, 8, 10, 12, 57br, 59, 81, 84, 85, 86, 87, 89, 90;
E.T. Archive, 47;
FM Modelmakers, 108, 109, 110;
Formech International Ltd., 119;
Roger Jackman/Oxford Scientific Films, 6br;
Margaret Turner, 6bl, 9;
Naim Audio Ltd., 91, 92;
Nordson,128r;
Pete Saloutos/ZEFA, cover;
Photoworks, 80;
President Office Furniture, 64, 70;
Racal Transcom, 57;
Techsoft UK Ltd., 105b;
Tony Stone Images/Michael Rosenfeld, 105t;
Wicksteed Leisure Ltd., 14, 15, 16, 18b, 19, 22tr, 22c, 22b,
30b, 33tr, 34tl.

Location and studio photography by Graham Portlock:
22tl, 25, 27, 29, 30t, 31, 34tr, 34b, 36, 38, 49, 50, 51, 52, 54, 65,
66, 69, 70, 73, 74, 75, 76, 77, 78, 106, 128l;
Chris Coggins, 56.

Contents

How to use this book   5

Case studies

Margaret Turner   6

Focusing on: the growth and development of a small company; developing a
corporate image through advertising and display materials using a company logo;
generating ideas for designs, and then modelling them; manufacturing small
batches and individual one-off items; the techniques of CAD, lost wax casting,
silver soldering, hand working and machining.

Wicksteed Leisure Limited   14

Focusing on: using British Standards to ensure product quality and safety;
developing mechanisms, materials and products with a focus on safety and
quality; how research findings and ergonomics help in developing play equipment
for different age groups; the advantages of modular systems and dimensional co-
ordination; assessing the environmental impact of a site or manufacturing
process; preparing and finishing components of wood and metal; designing jigs,
formers and fixtures for production; choosing the appropriate mechanical
fasteners or fabrication method.

Arcam   36

Focusing on: how understanding markets and having a product strategy may
suggest ideas for new products; developing a design brief; product development
planning – sequential engineering, scheduling and milestone planning; reducing
costs by modifying designs; influences on choice of materials, materials
processing, and fabrication methods; ways of organising production lines;
advertising and marketing.

Racal Transcom Limited   56

Focusing on: a specialist IT company that focuses particularly on design and
development of EFTPOS machines; how a brief for a new product is produced
through consultation with different users; the importance of teamwork in
developing a complex design; the use of CAD/CAM in manufacturing a mould for
thermoplastic injection moulding; how a fault that appears at a manufacturing
stage may be corrected by modifying the design.

President Office Furniture   *64*

Focusing on: teamwork between design consultants and a manufacturing company; developing an innovative product by analysing past products and by researching present user needs and emerging market trends; using models to present and test ideas, as prototypes, and as marketing tools; setting quality indicators for manufacture, and using computer-controlled equipment to check that materials meet them; preparation methods used with wood-based materials – sawing, veneering, routing, edging, surface finishing; using CNC machines in manufacture, including automatic safety features; flat pack furniture products and dimensional co-ordination.

Naim Audio Limited   *80*

Focusing on: stock control and production techniques in the manufacture of audio equipment; why decisions about the choice of specific materials within this field were made; an overview of the development of the company and its growth from very small foundations into a company that exports to customers all around the world.

General material

Product development   *93*

Materials   *111*

Fabrication   *123*

Glossary   *135*

Index   *140*

How to use this book

This book is in two parts.

The first part contains *case studies* about six companies. The case studies tell you how the companies design and manufacture their products, and the factors that they need to take into account. You will find a variety of activities and projects for you to tackle throughout the case studies. The activities will help you to understand the processes used by the companies. To help you find out more about the processes involved, there are references to the second part of the book which contains *general material* that applies to most of the case studies. Cross-references in this part of the book will enable you to see the processes in action in the case studies.

If you need to know what technical words and phrases mean, try turning to the *glossary*. In the main parts of the book these terms are shown in **bold** type.

We hope that you will enjoy reading the book and attempting the activities and projects.

Margaret Turner

Margaret Turner is a jeweller who designs, makes and sells her own work. She was interested in art from an early age but was frustrated at first because she could not draw very well. She was very relieved when she discovered that she could express herself as an artist by sculpting. The pleasure and freedom that she feels while working in three-dimensional media is reflected in the immense intricacy and detail in many of her designs.

Margaret studied at the Central St Martin's College of Art and Design in London. She was commended both for the quality of her work and also because at an exhibition of students' work she displayed and sold all her thirty pieces. Commissions poured in and so she needed to find a place to work. Her first workshop was the family coal cellar, which had been adapted by her father. She exhibited her work around the country at city art centres and galleries. The inspiration for her early work was largely animals and wildlife. Later she was inspired by Salisbury Cathedral and Westminster Abbey. Her recent 'Deep Sea' collection is based on seahorses, shellfish and starfish.

Margaret undertakes corporate commissions, and makes collectable items for individual clients. She also has a range which is produced in small batch numbers by casting methods. She believes that her jewellery must be 'comfortable, reflect the wearer's personality and give great enjoyment and satisfaction'.

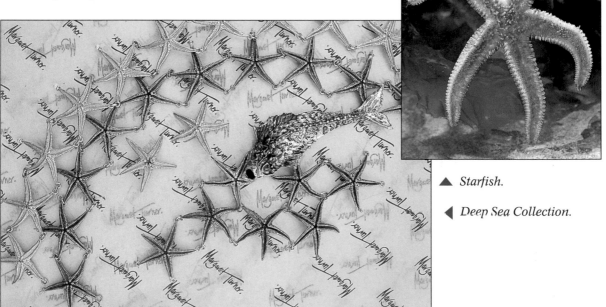

▲ Starfish.

◀ Deep Sea Collection.

Margaret decided that her jewellery would have the most appeal in a selective luxury market mainly for women. Most of her client base was built up by personal recommendation. Later, selective advertising was sent to clients on a mailing list.

Tunnard Design produced all the brochures, plans and information on which the company's public image is based. Chris Tunnard has also designed packaging, carrier bags, gift presentation packs and packaging tissue for the company.

In order to develop a **corporate logo**, Chris asked Margaret to sign her name a number of times. Chris computerised the signatures and created from them a logo which is used on all advertising and display materials.

▼ *Company logo.*

▼ *Chris generating advertising material on the computer.*

▲ *One-off items commissioned by Mr and Mrs Stokes. One ring was remodelled from three other rings belonging to Mrs Stokes. The candle sconces were made as a pair for Mr Stokes as a present for his wife. The cherubs were inspired by religious ideas and embellishments used on clocks. The business card holder was made from silver and gold for Mrs Stokes as a present for her husband. All the designs were generated after discussions between Margaret and the Stokes.*

Developing a company image

Margaret acquired her present gallery and workshop twelve years ago. A company was formed, which trades under the name 'Margaret Turner'. Business plans, covering both five-year and ten-year periods, have been written. This ensures that the company has both a direction and a target to aim for. It is well on target at the moment – Margaret has built up a company with a turnover in excess of £250 000 per year.

You try it ...
Design a logo by computer or other means which could form part of a corporate image.

More about ... using computers in design and manufacturing page 103.

Advertising material. ▶

Margaret and Chris have both produced advertising material for a show based upon the theme 'Trellis' which is being marketed to individuals and major fashion houses in a move to gain more access to a world-wide market. Margaret already exports to Japan and hopes to see her art taken up by fashion-conscious women and men, throughout the world.

Working as a team

This web diagram shows the contribution from various members of the team that works with the company. Each individual is responsible for their own area but is still part of the larger group. The team meets regularly so that everyone knows what is happening and can have a direct influence on decisions.

Margaret has overall control and is involved in every aspect of the business. She owns the company and is the main decision-maker as well as the designer.

Molly is concerned with **marketing** the jewellery in London.

Trish works in the shop, meets the customers and also sees to the general administration of the business.

Matt and Tamsin are in the workshops. They work in gold, silver, precious and semi-precious stones. They also undertake repair work for customers.

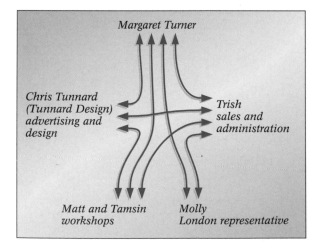

▲ *Web showing the interactions between members of the team.*

You try it ...
Draw a web to show how you interact with people you work with.

More about ... teams in industry page 101.

Designing jewellery

Generating ideas for designs

The designs are developed from different starting points. Some emerge from models Margaret makes in a three-dimensional medium. Others are developed from a series of sketches. Whichever starting point is chosen, a range of pieces (for example, a bracelet, ring and ear-rings) will have a common theme running through all the sketches. The design sketches are scaled to produce working drawings that are proportionally correct for the different items.

▼ *Design drawings for 'Trellis', 'Deep Sea' and 'Bubbles'.*

More about … selecting materials page 111.

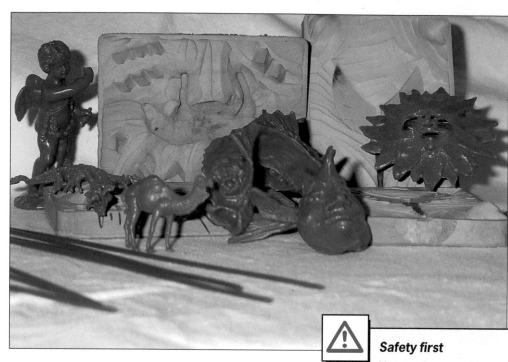

Moulds and waxes used in the casting of silver and gold.

Modelling the designs

Margaret models the items in a hard wax. She uses a spirit lamp to melt the wax into position for moulded areas. For detailed work she uses a soldering iron to melt the wax, and etches intricate shapes or textures into the work using dental probes and burs.

Safety first

Hot wax has a melting point of up to 200 °C. Always wear goggles and use gloves when handling this material.

More about ... casting page 118.
More about ... using models page 108.

You try it ...

Make models of the designs you have sketched. With some articles you may be able to form a casting by pouring hot wax directly onto it to give you both shape and texture. Negatives and positives can be made using plaster of paris, using a barrier to allow the moulds to be separated. (Put Vaseline onto it first so that you will be able to free the shape from the mould.) The plaster of paris could then be coloured to form a finished item.

Look carefully at your model and discuss its good and bad points with others. The following questions may help you to evaluate your model.
- Are there any sharp edges?
- Will it catch on clothes?
- Can it be improved in any way?

 *Small batch production*

Lost wax casting

Completed wax models are sent to London where the pieces are cast in metal using a lost wax casting technique. In this, the wax model is embedded in unvulcanised rubber which is then **vulcanised**. The mould is separated using a scalpel. This process requires a lot of skill as the two halves of the mould must fit together exactly after cutting to ensure castings taken from it are the same as the original. Wax is injected into the mould and a number of wax patterns are formed in this way. These are then made up into a 'tree' so that a single casting will give a number of identical pieces.

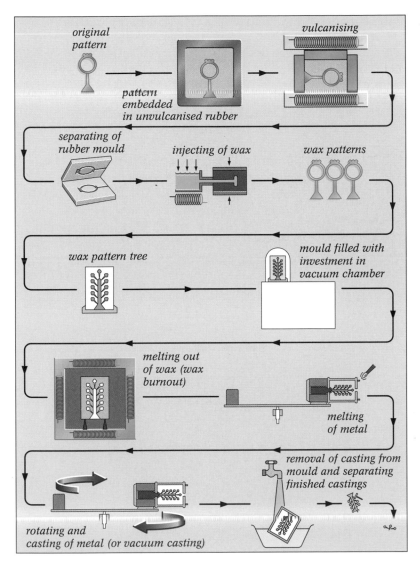

original
pattern

vulcanising

pattern
embedded
in unvulcanised rubber

separating of
rubber mould

injecting of wax

wax patterns

wax pattern tree

mould filled with
investment in
vacuum chamber

melting out
of wax (wax
burnout)

melting
of metal

removal of casting from
mould and separating
finished castings

rotating and
casting of metal (or vacuum casting)

◀ *Lost wax casting process.*

The **sprues** can be broken off and the individual items separated.

Checking and finishing the cast

The casts from the moulds are returned to the workshop. Matt and Tamsin have to check them to see that the quality is of a good standard and that all the detail is complete. The checks have to be very thorough to ensure that faults are corrected. Mistakes at this stage will be costly when the batch work is transferred into gold and silver.

More about ... quality page 98.

Once the checks are completed, the cast pieces are **fettled**. The casting is polished using a barrel polisher, which is a revolving drum containing polished steel grit. This process can take up to ten minutes.

The completed wax trees are placed in stainless steel flasks in a vacuum machine. The flasks are filled automatically with a solution called 'investment'. This liquid, which looks like plaster of paris, is left to set hard. The flasks are fired in a furnace at high temperatures so that the wax is melted away – this is why the process is called 'lost wax casting'.

The mould is placed in the casting machine and metal is injected. The mould is rotated to ensure that the centrifugal force throws the metal into the extremities of the mould. The casting is cooled, and the casting and mould separated.

Manufacturing the components

The finished piece can be used as a sample, and moulds can be produced using it as a **template**. The moulds can be used either for individual items or for small batch runs. Batch runs are needed when a repetitive theme is used – for example, for a bracelet or necklace. The moulds are sent to the casters in London, who produce the required number of castings in silver or gold. These castings are returned to the workshop for fettling and polishing.

Individual items such as rings, clips and fasteners, which are required to make up the finished jewellery, are made in the workshop.

Silver is drawn through a **drawing plate** which gives the desired diameter of wire. The silver is **work-hardened** during this process and needs to be softened by **annealing**. The metal is heated until it is a cherry-red colour and then quenched in water to cool it. The stresses and hardness are taken out of the metal during this process.

> ### You try it ...
>
> Work-harden copper by continually bending or hammering it. How does it change? Next, anneal the copper and compare the differences.
>
> Try this with other metals to see if they work-harden and anneal in the same way.

in water and placed in the barrel polisher to obtain a good finish. A final polish is given to the work using a buffing wheel.

Making individual items

Individual items and some one-off commissioned items are made in the workshop.

Some of the cast work may require additional handworked parts. These are made using basic materials such as sheet silver and silver wire. The materials are shaped and formed using hand-tools such as **planishing hammers** and stakes, saws and drawplates. Complex shapes can be built up by rolling, bending and shaping the material and by silver-soldering component parts together.

Fabrication

Silver soldering

The metal is joined using silver solder. Mountings for stones are added at this point. Silver solders have different melting temperatures which enables a second join to be made near to an initial join without the first one melting and breaking.

The first join is made using a hard-grade solder which has the highest melting temperature. The work will now have an oxidised coating caused by the flame. This needs to be cleaned off in the areas where second and subsequent soldering is going to take place.

Borax flux is applied using a small paintbrush, only placing the flux where the solder needs to go. If flux were put outside this area it would mean that the solder could flow onto other parts of the work causing damage or an unsightly finish.

The work is transferred to a bath of sulphuric acid to clean off any tarnishing caused by the heat, washed

Matt using a buffing wheel to polish an item of jewellery.

Tamsin soldering.

Some of the work produced is in different materials, for example silver and gold; these need to be worked separately through many of the processes before being joined together.

Textures can be added to surfaces which can give a more natural look to the finished product.

These processes are followed by cleaning in sulphuric acid and by buffing to make the product appealing and saleable to the public.

Safety first

Always wear goggles when machining.

Soldering requires good ventilation and the use of a borax flux when using silver solder.

Always wear goggles, rubber gloves and use tongs when using sulphuric acid. Wash everything in water after use.

When using buffing wheels always use the bottom quarter of the wheel so that if the work catches it is thrown away from you.

Hallmarking the metal for quality

The completed work is sent away for hallmarking. Hallmarking guarantees the quality of the metal (for example, sterling silver or 18 carat gold) because work which does not meet the assay requirements for metal quality will not be accepted for hallmarking. This can be the case if too much of a soft silver solder is used in the work.

More about ... quality page 98.

Inserting the stones

When the work returns any precious or semi-precious stones are fixed either by setting or, as is the case with costume jewellery, by using an adhesive.

More about ... adhesives page 127.

Summary

In this case study you have looked at:

- **the growth and development of a small company;**
- **developing a corporate image through advertising and display materials using a company logo;**
- **generating ideas for designs, and then modelling them;**
- **manufacturing small batches and individual one-off items;**
- **the techniques of CAD, lost wax casting, silver soldering, hand working and machining.**

You will now be able to complete the tasks below which may form part or all of your coursework.

1 Model a piece of jewellery in wax or other material.

2 Design and make an item based upon tessellations or on interlocking pieces so that a number of individual pieces are linked together to form the whole. (Use a template so that all pieces are the same.) You could also try combinations of materials to create contrasts and make the work more appealing.

3 Expensive jewellery is frequently manufactured using gold, silver and precious stones. Find out what other types of materials are used and to what effect. Apart from cost savings, what other reasons can you give to explain their use?

More about ... developing a specification for project work page 93.

Wicksteed Leisure Limited

Founded in the 1920s, Wicksteed Leisure Limited is a company that designs, manufactures and installs exciting playground equipment to the highest standards of safety.

▼ *Wicksteed is constantly developing new ideas for playground equipment, all with the aim of exercising children's imagination and senses, and different parts of the body. This is from Wicksteed's Rainbow range.*

Wicksteed's **market** includes public and private sectors in the UK and overseas. In the public sector, local authorities, government ministries and departments, and local parish and district councils are potentially customers. As pubs become more oriented towards families, the major brewery chains are an increasing sector of the market. This market is structured and partly seasonal, reflecting private-sector **specification** and buying procedures; January to March is the busiest period because it is just before the end of the financial year and the beginning of the next one in April.

Wicksteed uses several methods to market its products.

- It exhibits old and new products at trade shows.
- It sends out a large, detailed, full-colour catalogue to answer questions from potential and existing customers. The catalogue provides example playground layouts, detailed technical information, full product descriptions and recommendations.
- It supports the customer base by an active sales force.
- It has a comprehensive installation and after-sales service, which includes stocks of spare parts.

 *Meeting British Standards*

'Play hard, play safe'

Wicksteed's company slogan is 'Play hard, play safe'. To ensure that its products meet the demands made on them by children playing, Wicksteed takes great care with the quality of the materials used, the service offered, product safety, and the safety systems employed in the manufacturing process. This concentration on quality is reflected in the award to the company of BS 5750 – Wicksteed is a British Standard Institute (BSI) registered firm. The British Standards Institute regularly test products and manufacturing processes at Wicksteed against the Standards. A product that meets all the test requirements receives the BSI kitemark. Wicksteed holds more kitemarks and safety certification than any other manufacturer in their field.

▲ *BSI Registered Firm symbol.*

BSI kitemark. ▶

Classifying play equipment

By using BSI standards Wicksteed ensures that safety is built into all new products. The British Standard BS 5696: Part 2: 1986 *Play equipment intended for permanent installation outdoors* is central to virtually all the products that the company manufactures.

BS 5696 classifies types of play equipment as follows:

- static – no moving parts;
- agility – stationary structures such as climbing frames that allow users to balance, climb, swing and twist above ground level;
- moving – any piece of equipment with a moving part;
- rocking – the motion of the users depends on how they are supported on or between one or more pivots (fulcrum);
- rotating – equipment spins around a central axis;
- combined – includes both static and moving equipment.

Static play equipment. ▶

▲ *Agility play equipment.*

The equipment can be made up of three types of component parts:

- *permanent parts* are designed to last the life of the equipment;
- *consumable parts* are subject to wear and tear and can be expected to be renewed several times during the life cycle of the product;
- *replaceable parts*, whether permanent or consumable, can be easily replaced in situation.

The standard goes on to describe the design features of mechanical constructions and to specify sizes and angles of structural parts, safe finishes and fastening methods, as you will see later in this case study.

You try it ...

Look at the photographs of play equipment in this case study. How would you classify the different items? You might like to try classifying the equipment at a local playground, too.

Wicksteed products for younger children.

Designing playground systems

When designing playground systems that are safe but stimulating, Wicksteed take account of a number of factors. These include:

- careful choice of durable and safe materials;
- meeting the requirements of British and European safety standards;
- the positioning of items of equipment;
- the use of colour;
- incorporating natural landscape features;
- considering the age and ability of the children who will use a site;
- combating vandalism by careful choice of materials, fabrication methods, and fixtures and fittings.

Systems for younger children

Play is vital for most young children. They use toys, games, playground equipment and even empty cardboard boxes to help them play on their own or with others of a similar age.

Research suggests that children up to the age of three need:

- things to touch,
- textures to feel (every material has a recognisable quality to see and feel such as hard or squashy, smooth or fluffy),
- things to listen to, and
- things to watch.

Children aged three to five are very curious about their surroundings. They enjoy building and constructing things, painting, scribbling, sand and water. They like bright colours and shapes that have more detail. Toys and equipment for this age range need to be visually stimulating and fire the imagination by providing lots of ways to pretend and try out new ideas.

From the age of five children live in both school and home environments, and playing and working mean much the same. The range of play tools is broader – products such as playground equipment provide relaxation and fun. Over-fives are better at grouping and arranging things, from colours to shapes, letters and number. The type of play they engage in can be passive or active. They may drive the big red bus, be the conductor collecting fares or simply go along for the ride.

You try it …

Here is an extract from the European Safety Standard *Safety of Toys* BSEN 71; Paragraph 3.2:

2.5 Toys intended to be pulled along by the child.
Cords of toys intended to be pulled along, shall not include slip knots or fastenings likely to form a slip knot. In addition cords for toys for children under 36 months shall not be less than 1.5 mm thick.

Your company has been asked to design and make a mobile toy for children between the ages of 3 and 6. Use the headings below to produce a first specification for the toy which will be mostly used indoors.

- Sound
- Handling
- Colour
- Educational aspect
- Look
- Functional aspects
- Standard requirements

More about … developing a specification for project work page 93.

Modular play systems

If you talk to older people about what their playgrounds were like they will probably say that they had swings, roundabouts, slides and other separate pieces of stand-alone equipment. They may have made up their own circuits and challenges, and timed each other to see who was the fastest or most agile.

Wicksteed is one of the companies that have pioneered *modular* play systems. Each feature

▲ *A typical 1940s playground.*

installation worries about matching fitting and fixing holes. The manufacturer can standardise components, drilling and production techniques which avoids the need for stocking a large range of tooling and components.

> **More about ...** dimensional co-ordination
> page 106.

Rainbow range

In the Rainbow range for children aged 3 to 12, there are bridges, tunnels, ramps, ropes, portholes, ladders, climbers, puzzles, shop fronts and much more. These features connect at several different play levels to reflect the sizes and physical characteristics of the children using them.

The Rainbow platform or tower is the key structure for all **configurations**, providing the fixing point for the other parts of the system.

Non-slip platforms on towers, protective barriers and other important safety designs are built in as appropriate. The sub-systems, individual pieces of equipment, connect in a number of ways for use indoors or outdoors. Customers for the indoor equipment include supermarkets, leisure and activity centres.

in a modular system is fully compatible with the rest of the units in the range. This is made possible by the principle of **dimensional co-ordination** which was developed in the furniture industry, particularly in the area of fitted kitchen design. This enables customers to decide on the combinations they want based on the budget and the space available. If funds allow, more items can be added later with no

▼ *Products from the Rainbow range.*

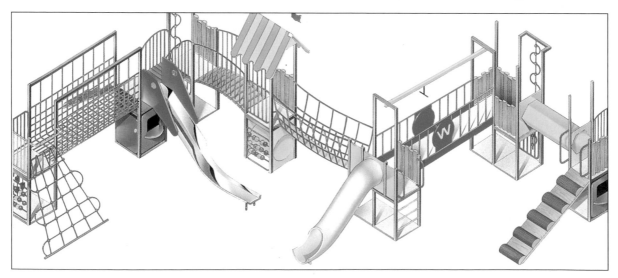

Discovery range

The Discovery range is designed for inner-city playground areas where usage is heavier, and uses strong and durable materials such as steel-reinforced ropes. Barriers to prevent children falling from or walking into hazardous areas feature the use of heavy-duty welded steel tubing or thermoformed polyethylene. Fibre-glass laminated in polyester resins replaces wooden roofs. This helps to reduce maintenance costs and the increase in strength extends the useful working life of the product. Tamper-proof fittings feature throughout all the systems in the Wicksteed range.

▲ *Products from the Discovery range.*

Logworld

Logworld is a robust multi-level play system built from softwoods taken from managed forests. Managed forests are those that have an active tree replacement programme.

▲ *The activity centre from Logworld.*

Ergonomics

Ergonomic considerations are key factors in product design. Ergonomics applies scientific information about humans to product development.

For example, most toddlers are physically smaller than primary school children. When playground equipment is being designed for a wide age range, things like the step height on a slide or the diameter of tubing on handrails need to be considered carefully. The designers have to know the range of acceptable sizes and constructional dimensions in order to fit the users. They may also decide to use an alternative to steps that toddlers find easier to use.

More about ... ergonomics page 94.

▼ *BS 5696 specifies the sizes and angles of ladders and ramps on play equipment. The measurements are based on anthropometric data.*

	Angle	Going A	Rise B	Treads	
				Depth C	Width
		mm	*mm*	*mm*	*mm*
	15° to 45°	220 min. 350 max.	100 min. 200 max.	Not less than A	600 min. 1800 max.
	45° to 55°	100 min. 220 max.	150 min. 200 max.	If open, not less than A If closed, not less than 150	280 min. 450 max.
			Spacing E	If open not less than 75 If closed not less than 150	230 min. 450 max.
	55° to 90°		175 min. 320 max.	Rungs diameter F* 25 min. 38 max.	
	15° to 38°		175 min. 360 max.		

All dimensions are in millimetres.

* It is essential that rungs are round or of other section with a top surface within the range of diameters specified and a maximum depth of 38 mm. NOTE. Angles are taken from the horizontal.

Figure 1. Permissible range of dimensions for straight access

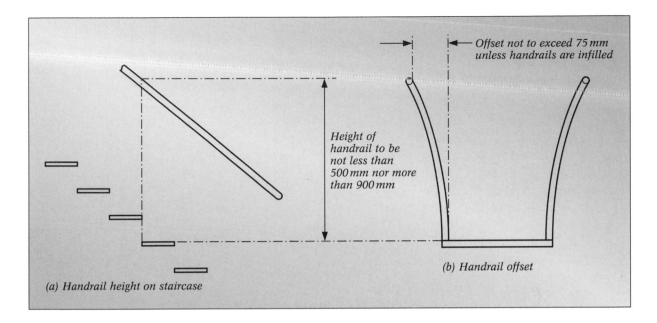

Offset not to exceed 75 mm
unless handrails are infilled

Height of
handrail to be
not less than
500 mm nor more
than 900 mm

(b) Handrail offset

(a) Handrail height on staircase

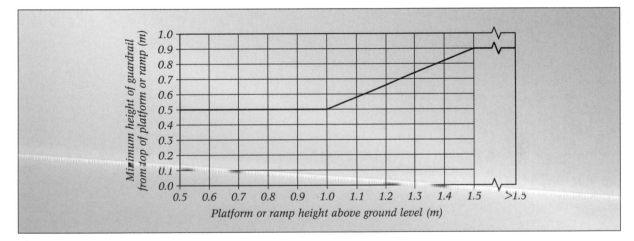

Minimum height of guardrail
from top of platform or ramp (m)

Platform or ramp height above ground level (m)

Designing safer equipment

Wicksteed takes care to design mechanisms that avoid common dangers. For example, speed restrictors are fitted to roundabouts for younger children to prevent the dangers of over-spinning. As the roundabout speeds up, an hydraulic device exerts an increasing pressure making it harder to push.

See-saws can be fitted with a non-bump mechanism to prevent them coming to a sudden stop which could easily lift a small child out its seat. Another design feature is that unlike 'spring type' see-saws they can never bump into the ground, which avoids the possibility of trapping fingers, arms or legs. Wicksteed have designed a completely enclosed interconnecting link mechanism for their non-bump see-saw.

Even with carefully designed equipment, children are still likely to take risks and fall from time to time. To help minimise injury in these cases, Wicksteed has designed a safety tile which can be used to make a safer surface underneath equipment. These are available in different thicknesses; the catalogue explains how to work out which thickness to use.

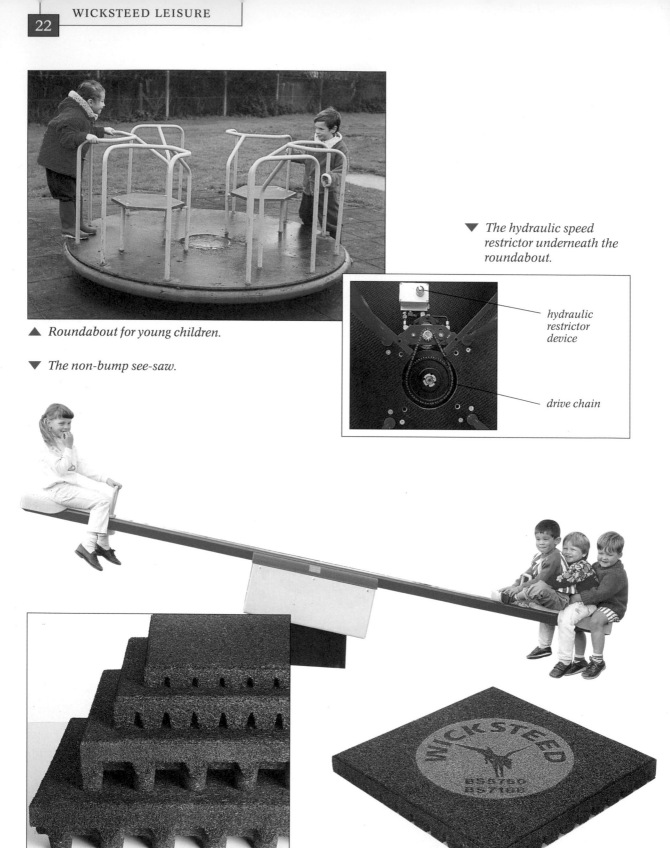

▲ *Roundabout for young children.*

▼ *The hydraulic speed restrictor underneath the roundabout.*

hydraulic restrictor device

drive chain

▼ *The non-bump see-saw.*

▲ *Wicksteed safety tiles.*

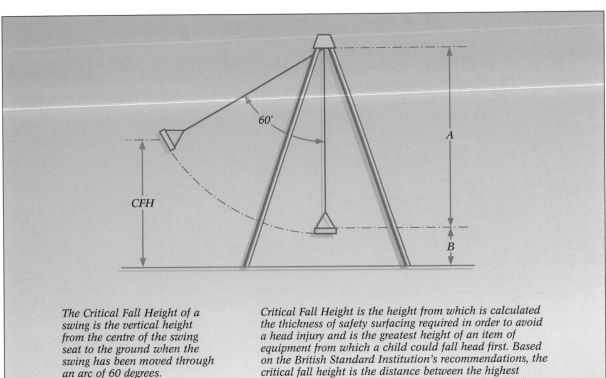

The Critical Fall Height of a swing is the vertical height from the centre of the swing seat to the ground when the swing has been moved through an arc of 60 degrees.

Critical Fall Height is the height from which is calculated the thickness of safety surfacing required in order to avoid a head injury and is the greatest height of an item of equipment from which a child could fall head first. Based on the British Standard Institution's recommendations, the critical fall height is the distance between the highest vertical accessible point of the equipment and the surface beneath and all Wicksteed's calculations are in accordance with these recommendations, as laid out in BS5696 Part 3.

CRITICAL FALL HEIGHT =
Half distance from Swing Seat to Swing Pivot (A) + Height of Swing Seat Surface at rest (B)

The diagram below shows the critical full height for each thickness of tile.

CRITICAL FALL HEIGHTS

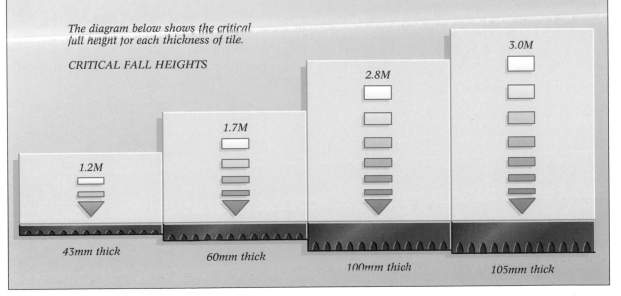

▲ Critical fall heights.

You try it ...

1 How do you think the hydraulic resistor on the roundabout works? What might the mechanism for a non-bump see-saw look like? You may need to visit a playground to do some practical research. Explain your ideas using block diagrams and models as appropriate.

2 Undertake a safety audit of a playground. Identify some of the potentially hazardous situations and how the designers of the playground have built in safety. Select one piece of equipment that you think could be made safer for either the user or people standing or passing by. Suggest, using words and pictures, how you would design it to be safer. For example, many swings do not have barriers attached to them to prevent other children running in front or behind the swing. The solution might be to fit low-level barriers that extend beyond the arc of the swing.

Environmental impact

Any product has an effect on the environment. Production processes can cause harmful emissions to the atmosphere and products can pollute the environment when they are disposed of at the end of their useful working life. Caring for the environment involves evaluating what effects activities may have on it.

All products have an **environmental impact** for their complete life cycle. Life cycle assessment, which is sometimes known as life cycle analysis (LCA), is one of the processes for evaluating environmental impact. The whole process of making a product from the raw materials stage through to its disposal has to be considered. A typical environmental evaluation covers energy and water management, and materials used (waste management and impact on humans).

Environmental impact assessment occurs at every stage during manufacture including the audit and monitoring of energy use, material use, waste disposal and environmental effects. The central points of any environmental policy are reduce, re-use, recycle.

Wicksteed are developing an active environmental policy using timber from managed forests, surface-finishing techniques that fall within British Standard environmental guidelines and safety tiles made from recycled tyre rubber.

▲ *Recycling symbol.*

1000 mm
(3'3")

▲ *One designer's solution to making swings safer.*

More about ...
developing a specification for project work page 93.

The environmental ▶ *impact of a product.*

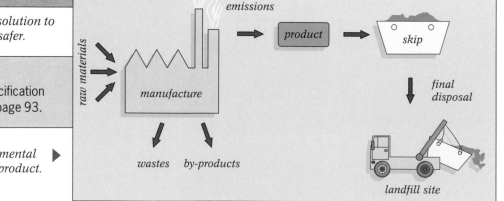

raw materials

manufacture

emissions

product

skip

wastes   by-products

final disposal

landfill site

Manufacturing the components

To ensure that the required quality is achieved in manufacturing Wicksteed's products, production engineers and designers often work together to develop manufacturing specifications. These specifications are used in discussions with outside companies that supply individual components and fastenings.

Preventing corrosion
Corrosion is a major problem for designers of play equipment. It can be reduced by:

● sealing a hollow section to prevent water getting into the section;
● making provision for water to drain away from the equipment;
● designing joints that are self-ventilating, self-draining or sealed to block water being drawn into the equipment by capillary action;
● avoiding connections between dissimilar metals to prevent **bi-metallic corrosion.**

One example of the impact of British Standard specifications at Wicksteed is the use of a 'baked-on' lead-free and cadmium-free paint finish on all the metal components. It replaces conventional gloss or wet spray paints.

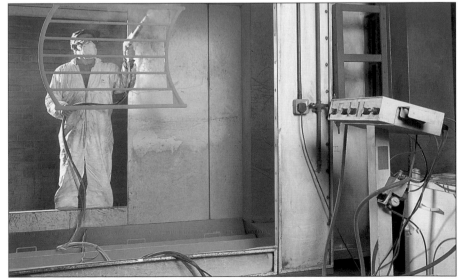

Spray paint booth. ▶ Polyester powder is electrostatically sprayed on to the shot blasted metal surface of structural pieces. Heating to 180 °C in a flow-through oven fuses it onto the surface.

Moisture content of wood for different uses. ▶

Moisture content %	Uses	
20	open-air seasoned wood	
18	outdoor and garden furniture	
16	garden tool handles	
14	bedroom furniture	
12	sports equipment	
10	living / dining room furniture	
8	hot conditions	
↓	too dry and brittle	

$$\% \text{ moisture content} = \frac{wet\ weight - dry\ weight}{dry\ weight} \times 100$$

In coastal areas, salty air can cause corrosion problems on metal-based products. The company offers the special option of undercoating with corrosion-resisting zinc spray. (This type of spray paint is readily available from shops selling accessories for cars and motor bikes.)

Preparing the wood for Logworld

Quality assurance also plays an important role in the manufacture of Logworld. Timber is a natural product which can warp or twist. To minimise the risk of this, Wicksteed specifies the use of softwoods that have been quarter-sawn to avoid unstable heartwood. Quarter-sawn boards have a distinct grain quality but are available in reduced widths and thicknesses. Though slash-sawn boards are wider, they are more likely to warp.

Timber should always have a moisture content which is appropriate to the environment it will be in. The timber for Logworld is air-dried rather than kiln-dried (which is a faster method). When a tree is sawn down it is in a 'green' state, 50 per cent or more of its weight is in the form of water. It is slowly dried in air until it reaches a moisture content of 18 to 20 per cent which is suitable for use outdoors.

Once the correct moisture content is reached the wood is pressure-treated with preservative to give a guaranteed life of fifteen years.

▼ *Quarter-sawn versus slash-sawn wood.*

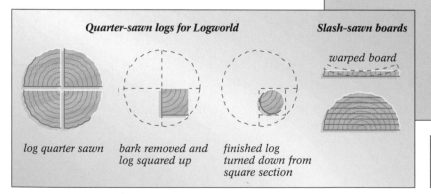

Quarter-sawn logs for Logworld   Slash-sawn boards

log quarter sawn   bark removed and log squared up   finished log turned down from square section

warped board

You try it ...

If you are using wood for your project that has been kiln-dried and stored inside a school storeroom it may have a low moisture content. Wood is a hydroscopic material – it can readily absorb or give off moisture throughout its useful life. If the product that you are designing will be in an outside environment, the wood may swell and warp in damp conditions. It can even shrink if it is in a very hot situation. You have to allow for this possibility in your choice of ways to make your product.

Experiment with off-cut pieces of wood stored in different conditions. Can you work out their moisture content?

More about ... wood
page 113.

Welding. ▶

Making metal components

The basic structure of most Wicksteed products is fabricated from tubular metal materials that are joined together using thermal joining methods. Steel is the main metal. **Fusion welding**, where the materials are heated until they melt and fuse together, is often the main method of joining.

Welding often involves the use of burning gases (for example oxyacetylene) or electric arcs. The decision on whether to use oxyacetylene or electric arc welding depends on the thickness of the metals being joined. If the thickness is up to 4 millimetres, oxyacetylene is used; if it is above 4 millimetres electric arc is used.

Joint preparation is critical to the success of any method of thermal joining. Wicksteed uses various types of joint on their metal structures, again depending on the thickness of the materials being joined.

▼ *Basic types of welded joint.*

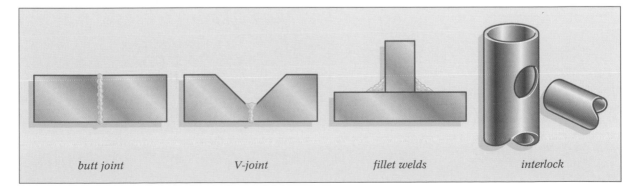

butt joint   *V-joint*   *fillet welds*   *interlock*

You try it ...

Make a simple butt joint in mild steel as shown. How could you compare the strength of a soft soldered joint and a brazed joint? Try out your ideas in the workshop.

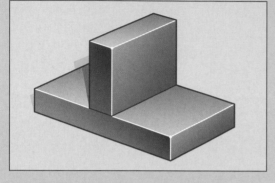

Butt joint in mild steel.

More about ... thermal fabrication page 127.

Safety first

Only undertake welding in a well-ventilated area under the close supervision of a qualified person. You must wear protective clothing and goggles. The goggles must be clearly marked with an appropriate British Standard number. Do not use oxyacetylene goggles to observe or undertake any form of electric arc welding.

Using jigs, fixtures and formers

Jigs, fixtures and formers are an important part of the manufacturing process at Wicksteed. They are production tools that enable parts, systems and structures to be produced quickly, accurately and repeatedly.

- Jigs guide production tools into the correct position on a workpiece.
- Fixtures are used to hold work securely and firmly to a machine table surface.
- Formers produce a particular shape or profile on a component.

Jigs

The most common types are drilling, bending and welding jigs. They can be simple plates with holes in them, or metal boxes or structures onto or into which components are located and clamped.

Drilling jigs

A drilling jig allows single or multiple holes to be drilled in workpieces that do not always present surfaces at right angles to a drill bit, for example, drilling into angled or irregularly shaped materials. They are also used to ensure that threading tools can be rapidly set up and used to cut screw threads in holes.

Drilling jigs. The jig for dowel holes could be made from mild steel for high-volume use or injection-moulded thermoplastic for low-volume use. The plate jig is used for locating and drilling larger pieces. ▶

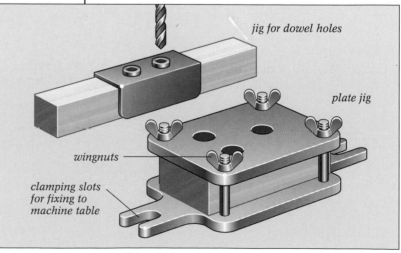

jig for dowel holes

plate jig

wingnuts

clamping slots for fixing to machine table

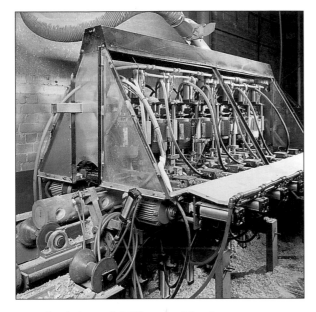

▲ *The dedicated drilling machine for Logworld at the Wicksteed Factory. Fixing holes are drilled from both sides of the log to avoid surface splitting and to ensure accurate location during installation.*

▲ *Hilmor tube bending machine in use at Wicksteed.*

Bending jigs

Bending jigs are used to secure and form materials to produce given bends. Tube bending devices produce bends in metal tube. They can also be set up to act as bending jigs, to produce multiple bends to set radii.

As the material is bent the outer surface of the bend is stretched, so allowance has to be made for the resulting movement of material as it bends. This is the bending allowance. Bending jigs also tend to be adjustable to allow accurate bending to different angles.

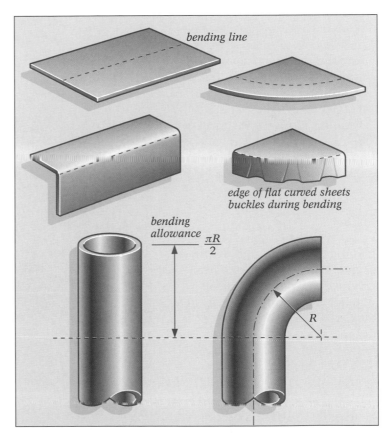

▲ *Bending different shapes; the bending allowance.*

▲ *A simple jig for checking the accuracy of the completed bend.*

Dedicated bending jigs are often used at Wicksteed – they allow the production of particular profiles or shapes. They can be quite simple constructions.

Welding jigs

A welding jig allows the rapid assembly and accurate location of the components that make up a joint.

Fixtures

Fixtures tend to be much stronger in design than jigs. They are used to hold work securely and firmly to a machine table surface on milling, lathe, grinding and similar machines. They often allow a number of machining operations to take place without having to take out and reposition the component. They are holding devices that do not guide a tool. Computer-controlled multiple tool manufacturing centres use fixtures to rotate the component

when the surface to be worked on cannot be reached in any other way.

At Wicksteed, assembly fixtures are used in the construction of particularly large structures such as the cantilever swing.

Formers

The way in which a former is used depends on the material being worked. The type and physical properties of a material determine the forces needed to form it into a shape.

Heat-formed thermoplastic components are used on certain parts of the Wicksteed range. The heated and softened thermoplastic needs to be lightly clamped until the plastic cools and hardens. The formers tend to be made out of hardwood. If the grain of the wood is raised, the former may be lined with a material like synthetic rubber strips. This is to prevent imperfections transferring to the surface of the component when it is heated and softened.

▼ *The Wicksteed cantilever swing.*

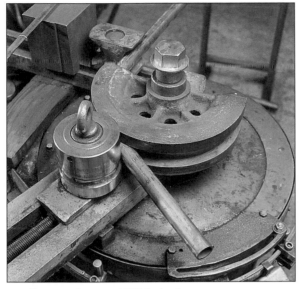

▲ *Formers in use at Wicksteed.*

You try it ...

Make a wooden former to produce the bends in strip acrylic to make the component shown.

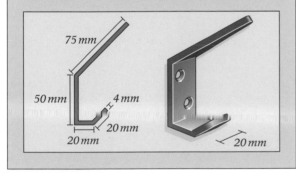

75 mm

50 mm 4 mm

20 mm

20 mm 20 mm

20 mm

More about ... forming page 119.

Designing jigs, fixtures and formers for production

Formers, jigs and fixtures save production time but need to be designed carefully. If the equipment does not produce accurate components, minor adjustments will continually have to be made. This will affect production time so that manufacturing costs increase. The development of additional **quality assurance** techniques is necessary to maintain product quality.

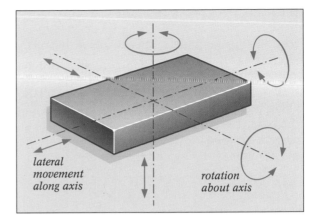

lateral
movement
along axis

rotation
about axis

▲ *The six degrees of freedom of movement for a cuboid.*

▼ *Types of movement in simple mechanisms.*

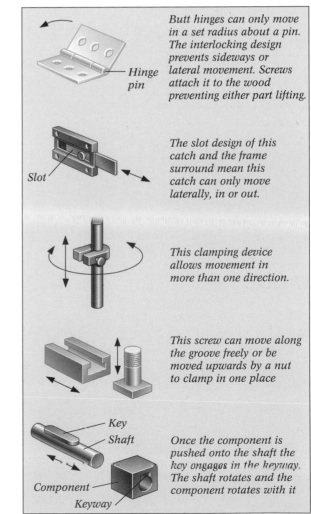

Hinge pin

Butt hinges can only move in a set radius about a pin. The interlocking design prevents sideways or lateral movement. Screws attach it to the wood preventing either part lifting.

Slot

The slot design of this catch and the frame surround mean this catch can only move laterally, in or out.

This clamping device allows movement in more than one direction.

This screw can move along the groove freely or be moved upwards by a nut to clamp in one place

Key
Shaft

Component
Keyway

Once the component is pushed onto the shaft the key engages in the keyway. The shaft rotates and the component rotates with it

When analysing the production of a required shape, you need to think about six degrees of freedom. For example, consider the design of a bending jig to produce a basic U-shaped component. It has to bend in two directions but the two bends are on the same horizontal plane, which is just one of the six degrees of freedom. The other five degrees of freedom have to be 'designed out' of the jig by using slots, clamps or other suitable holding and fixing methods.

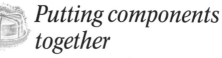

More about ... designing jigs, fixtures and formers page 121.

Putting components together

Wicksteed use a variety of fabrication methods which range from traditional wood screws to vandal-proof metal and plastic fasteners made to their own specifications by specialist manufacturers.

You try it ...

1   Why is this arrangement unsuitable as a drilling jig?

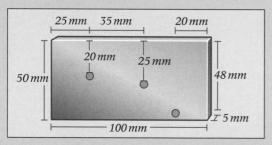

The unclamped V-block.

2   Design and make a jig that will hold a 100 mm × 50 mm × 5 mm piece of sheet metal so that holes with a diameter 6 mm can be drilled in the following places.

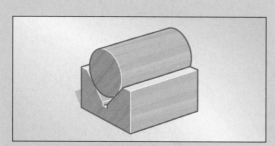

3   Design and make a jig to hold a mild steel tube with a 25 mm diameter so that a 6 mm hole can be drilled into it. The hole does not go all the way through the tube.

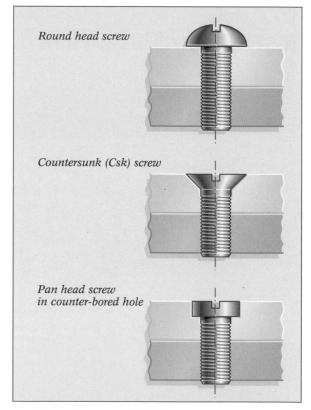

▲   *Types of screw suitable for play equipment.*

Fastenings are a potential source of danger to users of play equipment. Screws are usually round headed, countersunk or pan headed inside counter bored holes. Any excess threaded bar is cut off and 'peened' over to prevent injury. Shake-proof fastenings are used where there is any risk of loosening due to vibration or other types of force.

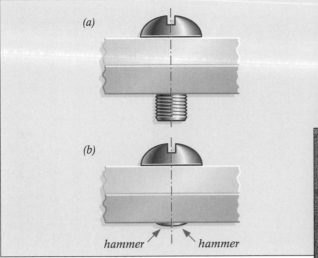

(a)

(b)

hammer   *hammer*

◀ *(a) If the threaded bar is too long, its sharp edges could injure children.*
(b) To prevent this, the excess bar is cut off and the end hammered (peened) over to remove sharp edges.

▼ *Tamper-proof fittings on Wicksteed products.*

Tamper-proof fittings are assembled using specialist tools. Socket-headed screws often have hexagonal-shaped holes. Wicksteed prefers to use socket screws with pentagon-shaped holes for security reasons. Pentagonal-shaped Allen keys are more difficult for vandals to find.

Improving designs

Lessons learned on one project can influence the design and manufacture of future products.

For example, the photographs on the next page show the step design on two different types of children's slide made by Wicksteed. In the first picture notice the number of separate components, parts and fixings needed to put the steps together. In the second design one sheet of perforated metal has replaced all the individual sections. The steps are formed by cold bending the sheet over specially shaped formers. The number of joins needed is reduced.

The second design is much safer. As well as the removal of sharp corners and edges, there is less chance of vandals taking any of the sections apart.

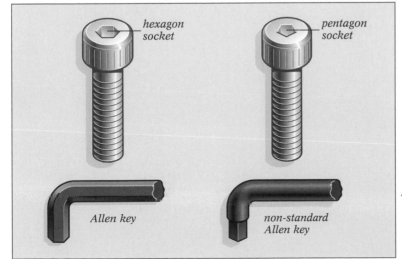

hexagon socket

pentagon socket

Allen key

non-standard Allen key

◀ *A traditional hexagon socket screw and a tamper-proof pentagon socket screw as used on Wicksteed equipment, together with their special Allen keys.*

▲ *The old step design has many components and fixings.*

▲ *The new design uses a seamless mesh and vandal-proof fixings.*

▼ *The new design was generated using CAD.*

You try it ...

Visit a playground. List and briefly describe all the pieces of equipment that you see. Include any seating or other facilities. Beside each item on your list write down the materials that you think were used to make it. Make a note of any specific design features that you notice.

Choose one of the smaller sized products in the playground to analyse in more detail. Make a list of all the different components that make it up. Work out the methods used to put the components of the product together. Answer the following questions for each component of the product.

- What material is it made from?
- Is it a solid, sheet or hollow construction?
- How does the individual part fit to, or join with, other components?
- Does the material affect the way this component joins to the other components?
- What sort of surface finish is applied to the component?
- Are there any obvious or visible faults in the component?

Suggest other ways of making the product or one of its component parts. Could you change the materials, the method of joining or the surface finish on the product?

Produce a short report using line drawings, photographs or other suitable graphical methods to explain your ideas.

Summary

In this case study you have looked at:

- **using British Standards to ensure product quality and safety;**
- **developing mechanisms, materials and products with a focus on safety and quality;**
- **how research findings and ergonomics help in developing play equipment for different age groups;**
- **the advantages of modular systems and dimensional co-ordination;**

- **assessing the environmental impact of a site or manufacturing process;**
- **preparing and finishing components of wood and metal;**
- **designing jigs, formers and fixtures for production;**
- **choosing the appropriate mechanical fasteners or fabrication method.**

You will now be able to complete the tasks below which may form part or all of your coursework.

1 A company is producing designs for a new range of playground equipment. One of the products in the proposed range is a simple bench seating unit. It will be a basic polymer-coated steel frame and weatherproofed hardwood construction. Assembly of the product will take place on site and may involve untrained people. Previous product experience and market research have identified that the durability and security of playground fixtures and fittings are key concerns for potential customers. What operational and service requirements would you include in the early discussions about the design and fabrication of this product? Compare your ideas with other people in your group. Between you produce an agreed list of general fabrication criteria (you could use the snowball technique described on page 102). Present your ideas in written and graphic form.

Use the criteria you have developed to produce an outline sketch of a design for the seating unit. Indicate the overall size of the unit. Identify and show the specific fabrication information for assembling the seating unit.

2 Design and make a range of small-scale play shapes for children aged between 5 and 7 years which can be used to simulate structures such as a railway station.

More about ... developing a specification for project work page 93.

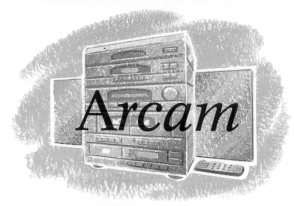

▲ *Arcam factory, purpose built for the company in 1980.*

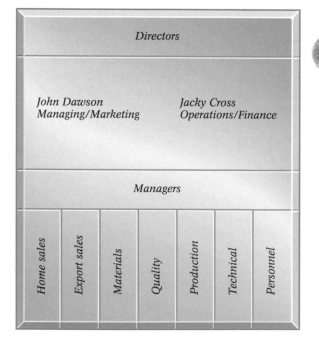

▲ *Arcam's management structure. The managers are specialists in their own areas but adopt a multi- or cross-functional approach to new product development and day-to-day operations.*

A&R Cambridge Limited, trading as Arcam, is a UK manufacturing company which employs over 120 people in the production of goods for the consumer hi-fi **market**.

Arcam designs and manufactures an affordable range of **amplifiers**, radio tuners, loudspeakers and compact disc (CD) players. The products are sold through a network of specialist dealers, which might be a small shop or large departmental chains. The export market accounts for one-third of sales. Arcam direct their **marketing** efforts at two sets of customers, the end users and the dealers in the retail outlets.

Looking at the market

Commercial design and product development are heavily influenced by business and economic considerations.

The marketing department at Arcam not only publicises the company and its range of products, but undertakes **market research** to ensure the company is offering the products that the markets want. Arcam undertake a considerable amount of market research. They rely on secondary research – mainly the specialist press and industry statistics. The analysis of a competitor's performance is done by model, range and by sector sales using readily available retail audit data. Primary research is through continuous and structured discussions with key dealers, distributors and the feedback/comment cards which are sent out with all their products.

You try it ...

Develop and design a survey form to provide information about a product that you are intending to design and make.

- What do you need to find out?
- How will you collect your information?
- How will you collate the data you collect?
- What methods will you use to analyse and evaluate the data?
- How will you report and present your findings? Will you use graphs, computer programs or other methods?

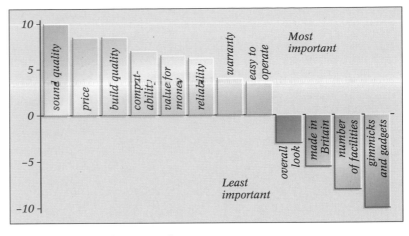

▲ *Results of market research into customers' preferences.*

The UK audio market

The 'static' (mains-powered) audio market in the UK is worth about £800 million per year at retail and is divided into three sections.

1	One-box systems	This section is dominated by own label and 'low cost' brands usually from the Far East. Sales volumes are high and profit margins low. Products generally have poor build quality and quality of sound. Retail outlets include high street multiples and mail order.
2	Mini/midi separates systems	This is the province of the major Japanese electronics brands. Prices are higher and distribution is through the high street and department stores. Although the quality of the product is perceived to be good, technically sound quality can be mediocre. The systems have lots of 'features' – some are functionally necessary, others are not. These systems have generally come to be seen as 'hi-fi'. Marketing is very competitive and reinforces the image of the product.
3	Full-size separates and loudspeakers (real hi-fi)	This is the sector Arcam have traditionally operated in. The sector is made up of the major Japanese companies and smaller specialists, including Naim Audio (see pages 80–92). The emphasis is on sound quality rather than gimmicks or give-away prices to establish a market share. The loudspeaker sector is largely dominated by British brands. Prices typically range from £150 to £1000 per single item.

More about ... market research page 97.

Audio markets are highly seasonal; sales peak in November and December and are usually at three times the levels of June and July, when people spend their money on holidays instead of hi-fi equipment.

You try it ...

1   Make a list of the types of market that you think Arcam are trying to create or satisfy.
2   Compile a simple chart to show those markets that exist all the year round and those that are seasonal in character. In what ways can information about its market help a manufacturing company (financial management, cash flow, phasing of manufacturing, loan financing)?
3   What opportunities are there for you to satisfy an existing market or to create a market for one of your own products?

Arcam's product strategy

Arcam believe that the broad range of products that they offer attracts both first time and repeat purchasers. The range also offers their customers an 'upgrade path'. If someone buys an amplifier one year, they may buy a CD player in the future. Brand loyalty is a crucial factor in ensuring continuing success.

The products offer high level technical design, a quality of sound and product build coupled with reliability at competitive prices. The company avoids gadgets and gimmicks.

Arcam's continued success depends upon having the right products on the market at the right time. They have three main elements to their product strategy.

1   Core business products – amplifiers and CD players, which generate 80% of the total turnover.
2   Non-core products – tuners and loudspeakers.
3   New product opportunities that can lead to new core markets.

The company realise that the life cycles of audio-based products are becoming shorter. To maintain competitiveness they have to improve their products on a one- or two-year cycle. They avoid the total redesign of their core products by evaluating, tweaking or modifying key parts of the electronic circuitry. The updating of a product image may be achieved by re-styling the front fascia panel and the layout of the controls.

By constructing a product matrix Arcam identified a gap in their product range – a CD player to retail under £300. From this, Arcam decided to design and manufacture a new product – the Alpha One CD player.

▼   *The Arcam product range.*

Product type	Price range (1993)	Arcam product	
		Alpha	Delta
Amplifiers	up to £250	✓	
	£250 – £350	✓	
	£350 – £500		✓
	£500 – £1000		✗
	£1000 – £1500		✓
CD players	up to £300	✗	
	£300 – £450	✓	
	£450 – £750		✓
	£750 – £1200		✓
Radio tuners	up to £250	✓	
	£250 – £400		✓
	over £400		
Nicam TV tuner			✓
Cassette decks			
Loudspeakers	up to £250	✗	
	£250 – £400		✓
	over £400		✓ (export only)

✗ identification gaps in product matrix

▲ The product matrix.

You try it ...

You can use charts like a product matrix to generate ideas or to structure your research and design work. Think about a general topic or market sector (for example, leisure equipment). List the types and range of products in that sector, their prices and where they are sold. This may provide you with lots of potential design ideas.

Developing the design brief

The first stage in developing a new product is usually a brief from management or marketing to the design team. The brief may vary in length and detail from a simple one- or two-line description to a lengthy document containing detailed performance requirements, costings and schedules. Here are some of the ideas that were included in the brief for the Alpha One CD player.

The Alpha One CD player is an entry point CD player. It will attract new customers to the Arcam brand name by offering the sound quality normally associated with the company, but at a more affordable price.

- The player must be a low-cost, high-volume product.
- There must be a minimal use of buttons and functions.
- The design must reflect the market need for quality and European styling.
- It must be easy to service, allowing access to the printed circuit board (PCB) and easy removal of electro-mechanical parts.
- Outside suppliers must be used as much as possible.
- All its parts must be supplied in 'finished' condition.

The design brief also specified:

- front panel controls, switches and heat sinks;
- dimensions, the overall sizes to conform with the European separates market;
- total cost figures.

You try it ...
The design brief checklist on this page is developed from industrial practice. Think about each item in the list – some might be useful directly to your work, others might not. Use the checklist to review the design brief for a product that you have already made.

Design brief checklist
Form of design brief
- verbal (spoken)
- written
- drawings

Information included in design brief
- evidence of actual or potential customer demand
- market sector and segments aimed at
- basic performance requirements
- target costs and selling price
- advantages over competing or existing products
- compatibility with existing products
- special or unique features of product
- guidelines on appearance, style and image
- relevant legislation, standards and codes of practice
- use made of standard components and assemblies
- requirements for ergonomics and safety
- potential for future adaptation or modification
- timetable and proposed completion/ launch date

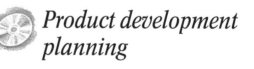

Product development planning

Sequential vs. concurrent engineering
When developing products in the past, Arcam like other companies used **sequential engineering**, a manufacturing system that relies on a linear sequencing of design and processing activities; work in progress is passed through a series of discrete self-contained stages. However, this system proved to be time consuming and an inefficient use of resources.

Arcam has now adopted **simultaneous engineering**, also called **concurrent engineering**, as a product development tool to improve manufacturing performance, quality and competitiveness. This uses a team-based approach to project management.

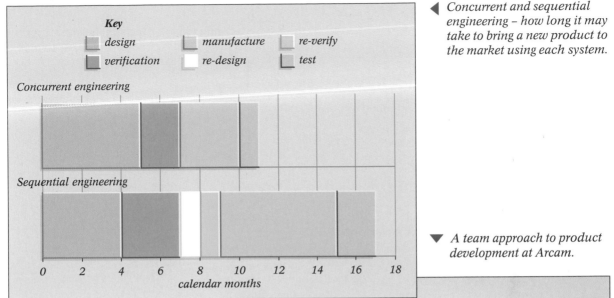

Key

- design
- verification
- manufacture
- re-design
- re-verify
- test

Concurrent engineering

Sequential engineering

0   2   4   6   8   10   12   14   16   18
calendar months

◀ Concurrent and sequential engineering – how long it may take to bring a new product to the market using each system.

▼ A team approach to product development at Arcam.

Sales and marketing

Operations managing director

Component suppliers

Dealers network

Technical

Product idea

Product discussion at Arcam

Quality

Production

Materials

A typical product development team now includes representatives from all the departments involved in taking the product from idea to market: sales, technical design, production, marketing, materials and quality.

For example, the production area makes sure the designer knows what factors make the product easy to manufacture and assemble – it comments on the *design for manufacturability*. The materials department's expertise helps to reduce the number of different parts, and to cut costs by increasing the number of parts that are also used in other products.

Arcam also involve their suppliers at an early stage. Suppliers can comment on which design options they would find easiest and cheapest to make and even offer alternatives that might be better. Using suppliers' knowledge of component life cycles and supply constraints means that Arcam does not design parts or components into the product that are about to be discontinued or will be difficult to obtain.

Arcam found that using concurrent engineering for the development of the Alpha One CD player gave the following benefits.

- The product was better designed and more easily manufactured because it had fewer components.
- There was a significant reduction in the time it took to bring the new product to market.
- Profit margins were improved.
- The product launch took place on time – a crucial factor in a demanding consumer-based market.
- New product development and manufacturing times have been cut substantially at a time when quality and company productivity have increased.

▼ *Stages from product brief to manufacture.*

Process	Key players
1 Develop idea for new product: • electronics design	Design department, and marketing and sales
2 Test the market position. • Will people buy it? • Who will buy it? • What is the competition? – market watching – technical and electronic features • Can it be made profitably for the selling price? • Does it match the company image and strategy? – aesthetic and visual judgements • Do the manufacturing resources match the requirements?	Technical manager, and marketing and sales
3 Create the design specification.	Technical manager, and marketing and sales
4 Form a concurrent product team.	
5 Make a milestone plan against which progress can be measured.	Concurrent product team
6 Define ideas on how the product will be built: • mechanical design • production drawings	Concurrent product team
7 Develop a more detailed and updated cost estimate.	Concurrent product team
8 Design and build a first working prototype.	Concurrent product team
9 Look at all ways to improve and develop the prototype: • technical testing	Concurrent product team
10 Second prototypes (3–5 players); selective market tests.	Concurrent product team
11 Improve and finalise design and method of assembly.	Concurrent product team
12 Small volume 'pre-production' manufacture (10–50 players).	Concurrent product team
13 Improve where necessary and then 'sign off' the design.	Concurrent product team
14 Volume manufacture.	Concurrent product team
15 Monitor quality and improve if required.	Concurrent product team

Preparing a milestone plan

The first thing the concurrent project team works on is to develop a milestone plan (see stage 5). This is a series of goals or '**milestones**', each of which must be achieved on time in order to achieve future milestones and finally the project objectives.

Milestones have to be carefully defined – that is, they must be 'robust'. This means that they should describe a real goal that can only be visited once, and without the achievement of previous milestones they should be impossible to meet. For example, 'final **prototype** available' is not a robust milestone as the prototype might not work. Additional time would be needed to put it right.

▼ *Milestone plan for Alpha One CD.*

PROJECT RESPONSIBILITY CHART			
PROJECT: **BUDGET CD PLAYER**			
Period: Week ending: *Approximately one year*	Issue date	Approved by:	
	M/S no.	Milestone description	M/S date	M/S leader
	CD1	Complete specification agreed		Design
	CD2	Concept / idea agreed		Design
	CD3	Key suppliers finalised		Materials
	CD4	First working prototype available		Design
	SD CD1	Sales forecast finalised		Sales
	CD5	4+4 working prototype accepted as correct		Design
	CD6	Parts list / kit agrees all suppliers fixed		Materials
	CD7	All components are in stock (100)		Materials
	SD CD2	Sales literature in stock		Sales
	SD CD3	Finished models accepted by sales		Sales
	CD8	100 models in stock		Production
	CD9	IEC and safety approvals granted		Design
	CD 10	Project objectives achieved		TEAM

In contrast, 'final prototype agreed correct' is a robust milestone. Obviously the prototype has to be available well before the milestone date so that any problems can be sorted out.

Milestones must also be 'required'. If any suggested milestone is not needed in order to achieve the project objectives, that milestone is deleted from the plan.

The milestones are discussed and agreed by the whole team. Each milestone becomes an objective in itself for a sub-project team who then identify the steps needed to reach their milestone. At that point another sub-project team might take over.

You try it ...

Look at the milestone plan produced by Arcam for the Alpha One CD player, then answer the questions below.

1 When does the company begin to plan the sales literature to support the new product? Is it at the beginning or end of the product development process?
2 At what point does the company begin to stock the components needed to make the product? Is it after the idea has been agreed or after the prototype has been made?
3 Each CD player is made up from a kit of parts. When is the parts list agreed in order to make up the kits of parts?
4 What three milestones are the sales team responsible for? (Look at the right-hand column.)
5 What manufacturing milestone is production engineering responsible for?
6 What milestones have to be reached before four working prototypes can start to be made?

Designing the product

Mechanical design is concerned with how the physical size of components affects other design parameters. For example, the casing of the CD player is 430 millimetres wide, to agree with industry standards.

Technical/electronics design is concerned with the circuitry and customised displays, and the availability and sourcing of standard electronic components. It also involves consideration of externally imposed constraints, such as the need to minimise radio interference to meet European regulations.

Industrial design considers aesthetic and visual judgement. The styling brief for the CD player, given to Cambridge Industrial Design, contains guidance on looks, and the needs and/or wants of users.

Technical testing involves testing the prototype. It also involves *environmental testing*, in particular testing in different climates for products that will be exported, and checking voltage differences. There will also be *functional testing*, which includes technical and listening tests, and *market testing* using the working prototypes.

▼ *Elements influencing design development.*

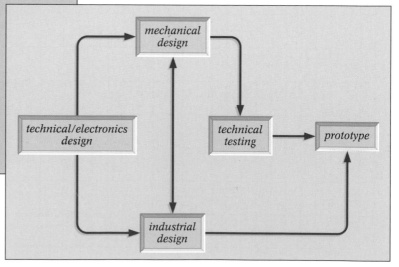

You try it ...

Select three products from the following list or choose three of your own.

- Rotary lawn mower – electrical
- Portable electric hand drill
- Hand-held battery-driven vacuum cleaner
- Jug kettle
- Personal CD player
- Hand-held computer game

For each product, identify at least two key features under each of these headings:

- Mechanical design
- Technical design
- Industrial design

Set out your findings like this:

Product	Portable radio
Mechanical design	(a) size of battery compartment to hold 4 × 1.5 volt batteries (b) a two-piece injected moulded plastic case
Technical design	(a) earphone socket (b) digital tuning device
Industrial design	(a) tuning display panel (b) style and colour of lettering

Now choose just one of the products and produce a simple block diagram to describe how the mechanical or electrical system works.

Reducing costs by design

Manufacturing electronic products usually involves the assembly of different systems, sub-systems and components in a range of resistant materials to meet specific design specifications. This process is known as *fabrication*. Designers and production engineers are often faced with the problem of joining parts made out of different materials. They have to consider the relationship between service, mechanical design, product safety and specific customer requirements.

The mechanical design of the original Arcam Alpha amplifier, which was designed in 1982, illustrates this. In the audio market components and circuit boards are getting smaller in size all the time. This means that products could be made smaller and lighter. Customers in this sector do not like the equipment to have hardboard or cardboard panels, though from a design point of view these panels can perform the required operational functions of holding connection devices, plugs and sockets reasonably well and provide a cheaper alternative to a steel or aluminium panel.

Arcam needed to bring their amplifier in at an 'entry point' cost because it was aimed at the lower-priced end of the 'quality' hi-fi separates market. They needed to make an operating profit but they had to satisfy the customer preferences expressed in the market research data. They based the design of the case around the use of low cost extruded aluminium end pieces made by a specialist supplier. This meant the case could be made up like a picture frame without the need for drilling or tapping screw threads. It was an award-winning innovative design.

There were some problems with using aluminium **extrusions.** When Arcam placed an order for extrusions, it took over six weeks for the supplier to deliver, a second company then cut the extrusion to the required length, and a third company painted it. In all, the total time from order to delivery of finished parts was over nine weeks. Arcam had to predict demand that far ahead, in a seasonal business, and this was very difficult.

When the time came for Arcam to re-style and update the original Alpha series products, they made a change from a case design made of aluminium extrusions to a sheet metal construction.

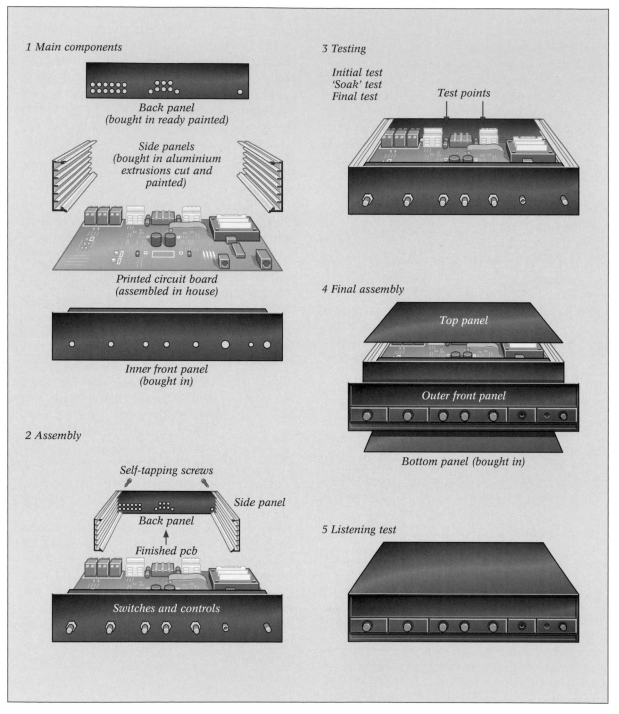

1 Main components

Back panel
(bought in ready painted)

Side panels
(bought in aluminium
extrusions cut and
painted)

Printed circuit board
(assembled in house)

Inner front panel
(bought in)

2 Assembly

Self-tapping screws

Side panel

Back panel

Finished pcb

Switches and controls

3 Testing

Initial test
'Soak' test
Final test

Test points

4 Final assembly

Top panel

Outer front panel

Bottom panel (bought in)

5 Listening test

▲ *Assembly of the original Arcam Alpha amplifier. The PCB is held in the channels of the extrusions. The front and back panels are held by self-tapping screws that fix into the other extrusions. The top and bottom of the case are screwed on last, which allows access for PCB testing throughout the assembly operation. It is also an important time-saving feature for service engineers in the unlikely event that the product develops a fault.*

The supplier, West Hyde Enclosures, can manufacture the new case parts in three weeks from sheet metal which is readily available off the shelf. Other benefits gained in the new design were fewer parts, a faster assembly time, and the use of fewer raw materials. A change from the smooth to a textured paint finish on the case reduced the effects of damage during assembly and, overall, a slimmer and more aesthetically pleasing design was achieved. By re-designing the case Arcam have speeded up production, reduced their manufacturing costs and increased the overall profitability of this product.

You try it ...

1   Look at a number of household objects that have been mass produced. What design decisions have been made to reduce costs?

2   Look at the 1930s radio shown here. Could such objects be mass produced now? What problems might there be?

◀ *A Philips 1933 radio.*

▼

Designing the Alpha One CD player chassis

The specialist firm West Hyde Enclosures was sub-contracted to produce the chassis case as well as the front and rear panels for the Alpha One CD. The way that Arcam involves its suppliers meant that the Senior Design Engineer for West Hyde was involved in the design discussions virtually from the start.

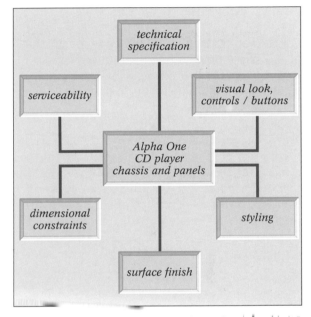

▲ *Design issues for chassis and panels of the Alpha One CD player.*

Choosing materials

The structural purpose of the chassis is to support the player mechanism and associated electronics. No great strength is involved but rigidity is important.

The options were:

● galvanised sheet steel of minimal thickness or gauge (cheapest option);

● steel of a bigger gauge;

● aluminium, which has better heat dissipation characteristics (this is important in electronic products).

Market research had shown the perceived value that weight gives to this class of product. Cheaper panel options such as hardboard were not considered viable on a product in this sector of the market – Arcam have a brand image to maintain.

The choice was a heavier gauge of steel than was needed from a structural point of view. From a cost-benefit point of view the customer's feeling of value for money was seen to balance and offset the cost of the extra weight of material involved.

For the top cover, aluminium was chosen for its heat dissipation qualities. Aluminium has a dampening effect, it reduces vibrations and is less resonant than steel. This makes the product sound better.

The decision was made to use the same design of lid as on the amplifier in the same product range. This significantly reduced the tooling and processing costs. This is known as **component standardisation**. The choice of aluminium also reduced overall finishing costs.

> **You try it ...**
> Why is rigidity important in the materials chosen for the chassis? Test various materials for strength and rigidity and write a report on your findings.

> **More about ...** materials page 111.

Choosing surface finishes for panels

The rear panel contains all the connectors, low voltage inputs and outputs, mains connection, user information and warning labels. The panel is painted black. It is a 'flat' finish to allow for the silk screen printing of the information about connections and sockets.

The 'gloss-level' of the other, plastic-coated panels was seen to be important. The choice was between a flat, shiny finish and a fine-textured paint. Factors considered were:

- the durability of the finish in use – one surface finish wears more evenly than the other;
- dust in the air – one finish does not show the dust as much as the other;
- covering defects – one finish shows imperfections in the manufacturing process and scratches more clearly than another, which means there will be a much larger number of reject panels.

> **You try it ...**
> What choice of surface finish would you make? Use a range of paint finishes on pieces of metal and compare them using the criteria above.

> **More about ...** finishing processes page 118.

Chassis design

Arcam decided to use a virtually flat perforated steel sheet that is easily folded into shape without the use of costly bending equipment – this matches the other products in the Alpha range.

Originally Arcam received cases already folded. These occupied space when they were shipped – the company was paying to transport empty space – and once the packs arrived at the factory they also needed a large area for storage. West Hyde now supply the chassis in 'flat packs'.

Making the chassis

Once the chassis design was underway West Hyde Enclosures had to decide how they would manufacture it.

The options were:

- a press tool – if they used a composite tool they could complete the operation 'in one hit';
- a **CNC** machine using a carousel of special tools to produce the holes and shapes required.

The press tool would be high in cost (up to

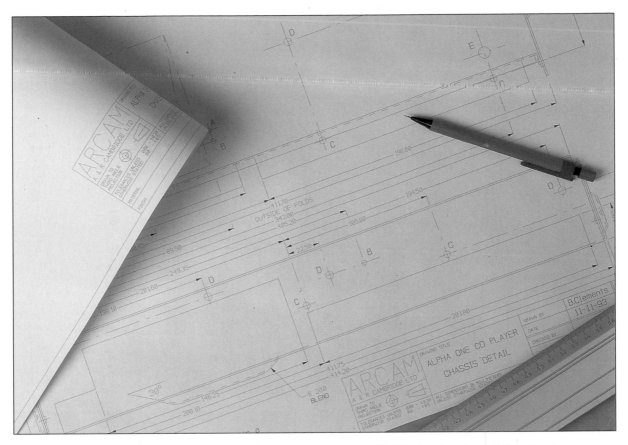

Detailed design drawings of the chassis.

£10 000) but that investment results in a low **piece part** cost. The problems were the likely sales volume of the product and the time scales involved. CNC provides a flexible 'soft tooling' option (soft tooling because standard cutting tools could be used rather than the more expensive press tool). This method allows for any future change in technical design such as re-positioning of slots or holes. The problem is that the piece part cost is higher so the price Arcam are charged is higher.

The choice was between a high tooling cost or a high piece part cost.

> **You try it ...**
> Which option would you choose and why?

> **More about ...** using computers in design and manufacturing page 103.

Putting the chassis together

One of the problems Arcam always have to overcome is how to join thin sheet materials using mechanical fasteners such as screws and nuts. From an engineering point of view it is difficult to put a thread into a thin sheet of metal. There isn't enough thickness of material to get the required number of threads in, usually at least three. The threads can easily be 'stripped out' and the chassis quickly becomes useless and (more importantly) unsafe.

On large products the problem is solved by soldering, brazing or welding an ordinary nut inside the case which provides the correct number of threads and therefore a more secure fastening. However, if Arcam settled for this solution it would cost them a considerable amount of money to buy the nut and then have it skilfully fixed in place.

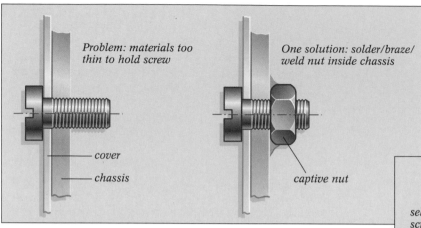

Problem: materials too thin to hold screw

One solution: solder/braze/weld nut inside chassis

cover

chassis

captive nut

◀ In thin sheets of metal there is not enough thickness of material to screw into.

▼ By pressing the fixing hole, a flange is formed which gives the thickness needed for self-tapping screws to work effectively.

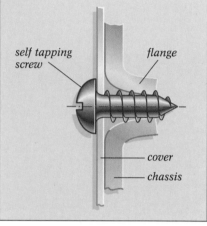

self tapping screw

flange

cover

chassis

Arcam and West Hyde Enclosures devised a technique which is used during the manufacture of the chassis. Compared with other methods this costs 90% less for each of the screw fittings on the chassis.

More about ... mechanical fasteners page 124.

Production at Arcam

Arcam produce 25 000 to 30 000 audio separates per year. These figures for volume of product do not always justify costly investment in fully automated assembly equipment. The company is introducing some automatic and semi-automatic production aids.

A piece of 'directed assembly' equipment helps to put some of the electronic components in place on the printed circuit board (PCB). This is known as 'populating' the PCB.

A flow solder machine is used in the final production of the PCB.

At Arcam the main thermal fabrication method is soft soldering; this provides a physical contact and electrical conductivity. The solder is a tin–lead mix. The relative proportions of tin and lead vary but are related to the amount of 'flow' required and the capacity to dissipate heat quickly to prevent the overheating of delicate electronic components.

▲ Directed assembly equipment.

▲ *Flow solder machine.*

Build quality and product reliability are made possible by the use of a manufacturing defects analyser (MDA) and computerised automatic test equipment (ATE) in a dedicated test and soak area where selected units from a batch are tested over time. This is known as burn in.

The last test on every item is a listening test using standard discs and tapes.

Different ways of operating production lines
Arcam have operated their production lines in a number of ways.

In *line production* the product is assembled by passing through a sequenced series of single operation workstations.

In *cell production* the product is assembled by a team of people. Anyone in the team at Arcam can do any of the assembly functions. The idea of cell working has grown in popularity throughout Arcam. The company sees the idea of group responsibility as a key way of improving product quality. It also fits in with their concurrent engineering approach.

You try it ...
Electrical solder has to melt and then solidify very quickly because heat damages electronic components. From the graph, what mix of tin and lead is best for soldering electronic circuits?

More about ... thermal fabrication page 127.

The melting characteristics ▶ *of tin–lead alloys.*

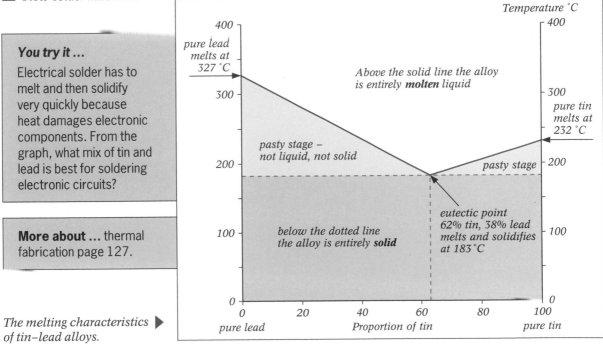

Manufacturing the Alpha One CD player

Process	Requires
Inspect PCB	PCB
Functional test	Automatic test equipment
Assemble in case	Case and CD mechanism
Burn in	10% of batch
Final test and listen	Complete product
Pack	Packaging materials

▲ *Manufacturing processes on site: an overview.*

Production line. ▶

▼ *Planned production line for Alpha One CD player.*

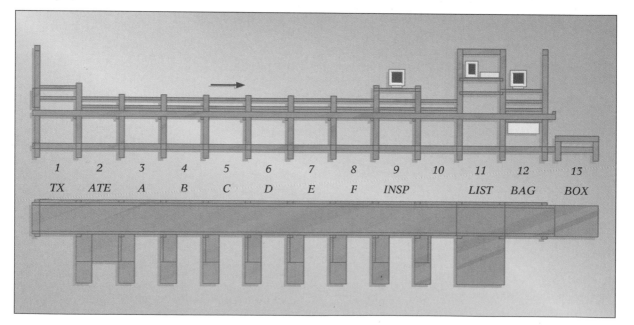

1	2	3	4	5	6	7	8	9	10	11	12	13
TX	ATE	A	B	C	D	E	F	INSP		LIST	BAG	BOX

Line position		Time
Line position 1	Place transformer on PCB, secure with tie wrap and solder. Fit voltage label on transformer.	1 min 30 s
Line position 2	Place PCB on automated test jig. Run test.	3 min 10 s
Line position 3	Prepare chassis – bend to shape – fix warning label. Add feet, fixing pillars, PCB insulator, acoustic damping pad. Secure PCB with screws. Plug in display to PCB.	2 min 30 s
Line position 4	Secure earth lead to CD mechanism – screw and crinkle washers. Fit CD mechanism to chassis – four snap rivets. Remove protective plastic film from LCD display. Secure gaskets and windows over display. Check display operation. Fit laser warning label to outside of chassis.	1 min 58 s
Line position 5	Fit buttons. Fix front panel to chassis with fasteners.	2 min 44 s
Line position 6	Fit rear panel to bottom of chassis using 2 washers and 2 screws. Secure phono connecting socket to rear panel with 2 screws. Secure connectors and phono sockets to rear panel with 4 screws. Fit blanking rivet into earth hole above mains inlet. Fit laser label to space provided on rear panel.	2 min 40 s
Line position 7	Repairs bench.	
Line position 8	Pass unit onto the off soak test area for testing.	
Line position 9	Fit cover gasket to CD drawer mechanism. Front panel check. Voltage/bar code labels. Inspect the unit – internal check and rear panel check.	1 min 39 s
Line position 10	Fit cover plate to chassis. Use 4 screws for the chassis side and 4 for the rear panel. Check alignment of chassis.	1 min 30 s
Line position 11	Listening test.	3 min 5 s
Line position 12	Clean the unit. Put in polythene bag and add documentation and accessory pack.	2 min 40 s
Line position 13	Box and dispatch.	
Total time for unit		**23 min 26 s**

Advertising and marketing

An outside advertising agency provides expertise and advice on all aspects of Arcam's marketing strategies including press advertising, public relations, company image, and the development of a direct-mail system. Sales managers with responsibility for home and export sales also play an important role in maximising product demand. The dealers are most important to the company because they can exert considerable influence over the customer. The specialist industry press and consumer magazines are kept up to date with product information. Reviews are taken seriously and are actively addressed when products are upgraded. Favourable reviews and industry awards are all strong opinion formers in buyers' minds.

Arcam use a variety of techniques to promote their products:

- advertising (most adverts include a reader response contact number);
- public relations exercises;
- trade and public exhibitions around the world;
- distribution of product literature and product reviews;
- direct mail targeted at existing and potential customers and dealer contacts.

> **You try it ...**
> Describe the features that might go into the marketing of a new washing machine.

Summary

In this case study you have looked at:

- **how understanding markets and having a product strategy may suggest ideas for new products;**
- **developing a design brief;**
- **product development planning – sequential engineering, scheduling and milestone planning;**
- **reducing costs by modifying designs;**
- **influences on choice of materials, materials processing, and fabrication methods;**
- **ways of organising production lines;**
- **advertising and marketing.**

▲ Reviews.

You will now be able to complete the tasks below which may form part or all of your coursework.

1 You are an industrial designer. You have been given a brief to design the fascias for a portable cassette player for young children. Invent a cartoon character and produce a full-size layout for the cassette player which incorporates your character. Look at existing cassette recorders to help you to produce the measurements.

2 A company working for a chain of charity shops has produced designs for a low-cost, free-standing wooden shelf for storing small storage jars in a domestic kitchen. It is a self-assembly slot-together flat pack design. The outline design is shown below.

- Produce an outline plan identifying the main cutting and assembly stages clearly.
- Make recommendations about the methods of organising a simple production line.
- Test and model your production line using suitable materials.
- Make any necessary modifications to your proposal.
- Present your final ideas in a suitable form for discussion at a team meeting.

3 Think of a product you would like to make. Use the design brief checklist on page 40 to produce a design brief. Then plan how you could develop and make it.

- Identify the key tasks that need to be done.

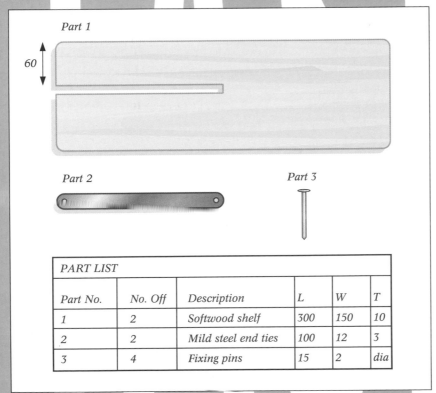

◄ Parts for the self-assembly slot-together free-standing storage shelf.

Part 1

60

Part 2   Part 3

PART LIST					
Part No.	No. Off	Description	L	W	T
1	2	Softwood shelf	300	150	10
2	2	Mild steel end ties	100	12	3
3	4	Fixing pins	15	2	dia

Your task is to assume the role of the production manager in the company which will manufacture the product for the charity shop.

- Produce a three-dimensional view of what the assembled shelf will look like.

- Develop a timetable that will use your project time as effectively as possible.
- Draw up a milestone plan for your product.

More about ... developing a specification for project work page 93.

Racal Transcom

Racal Transcom is a company which specialises in information technology (IT). It is an autonomous company within the Data Communications Group of Racal Electronics plc. The company was formed in 1980 specifically to provide equipment to support the emerging **EFTPOS** (electronic funds transfer at point of sale) market.

If you visit a shop and pay for goods using a plastic card, your card is swiped through a reading head, the transaction is recorded and the amount you have spent is either debited from your account at that instant or debited against your credit card account, for example Access or Visa Delta. This system means you do not need to carry large amounts of cash around, and gives you the flexibility to purchase goods at any time.

Racal Transcom is the UK's leading manufacturer of EFTPOS terminal equipment and has sold in excess of 100 000 electronic data capture and authorisation terminals to the UK market. Customers of Racal Transcom Ltd include Barclays Bank plc, National Westminster Bank plc, Lloyds Bank plc, Bank of Scotland, Co-operative Bank plc, the Burton Group, American Express and The Diners Club Ltd.

▼ *Using an EFTPOS machine in a small shop.*

You try it ...

1 What types of machines do businesses use for plastic card transactions?
2 Do a survey of where retailers or other outlets have EFTPOS machines. What benefits do the retailers see in using them?

More about ... market research page 97.

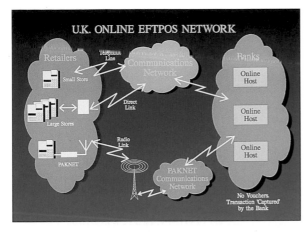

▲ *The EFTPOS network in the United Kingdom.*

Focusing on design and development

Racal Transcom designs, manufactures and supports terminals for EFTPOS, together with a range of ancillary equipment. The company employs over 100 people. More than a quarter of these are concerned with design and development.

The company sees its role as contributing to the development of EFTPOS, rather than merely exploiting the commercial opportunities presented by the market. It maintains direct contact with, and seeks to understand the motivation of, all parties interested in and

▼ *Working together to develop EFTPOS.*

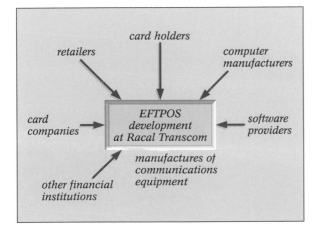

contributing to the development of EFTPOS. It uses the insight provided by these contacts to guide product development, almost all of which is funded by the company. The aim is to spend about 10 per cent of annual turnover on development projects. In the early years before the EFTPOS market began to take off this proportion was substantially larger.

Product development is a continuous process, reflecting the steady evolution of the EFTPOS concept. Although the company is happy to discuss customising their products to meet individual customer requirements, they believe that funding basic product development themselves encourages the development of products that better meet the needs of the market as a whole.

The product Cardmate 2

Cardmate 2 is one of a number of products which have been designed and produced by the company. The machine is compact, simple to use and install which makes it ideal for a variety of retail environments including lower volume outlets. A *lower volume outlet* is a retail environment where business is small (for example, a small hotel) which has customers needing to use cards for some purchases. These businesses would previously have used a paper-and-roller machine to process card payments.

Cardmate 2 offers the retailer a cost-effective electronic system for all credit and debit card

▼ *Cardmate 2.*

transactions which includes an immediate transaction authorisation facility. Cardmate 2 has a simple 'plug-in-and-go' installation procedure where all configuring and host computer log-on transactions are performed automatically. All that is needed is a **modem**.

User-friendly prompts on the Cardmate 2 display guide the operator through each transaction. The card is swiped through the reading head, the amount keyed in and the Cardmate 2 contacts the appropriate bank computer automatically. The machine prints a two-copy receipt for the customer to sign, complete with authorisation code. The transaction is sent to the bank electronically.

The rest of this case study looks at how Cardmate 2 was developed.

One of the major problems associated with earlier EFTPOS machines was the requirement for an engineer to go out to install the machine and teach the retail staff how to use it. It was part of the new brief to try to eliminate this problem. This would enable more machines to be sent out and would be far less costly in engineers' time and salaries.

Because of the limited space available on the counters of small retailers, the machine's *footprint* (area needed) had to be kept as small as possible. A further consideration was the final cost of the new machine. Existing machines were expensive and many smaller retailers could not afford them. Cardmate 2 had to be affordable by smaller retailers.

You try it …

What information would a bank need to know? Produce a flow chart of the process of accessing information, from swiping the card to final authorisation.

Perhaps you could watch a few transactions taking place and note any differences in procedures.

From design to manufacture

Because of the complexity of the project and the range of skills needed in its development, a design team worked on the project rather than

▼ *Web showing interactions between the team members and their responsibilities.*

Developing a brief

The need for the project was established from previous work carried out by the company for banks. Most credit-card transactions done by small retailers used paper and duplicated information which then had to be sent to the banks to be recorded on their accounts. This was time-consuming and expensive for both banks and retailers, and could not debit accounts at the point of sale. A new machine was needed to allow transactions to be sent to the banks electronically at the point of sale.

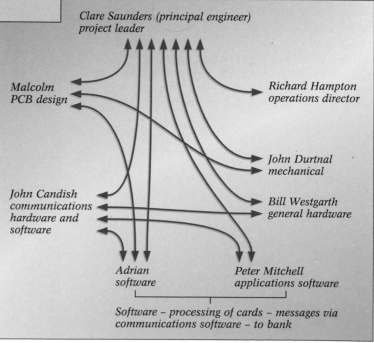

Clare Saunders (principal engineer) project leader

Malcolm PCB design

Richard Hampton operations director

John Durtnal mechanical

John Candish communications hardware and software

Bill Westgarth general hardware

Adrian software

Peter Mitchell applications software

Software – processing of cards – messages via communications software – to bank

just one individual. The person chosen to be the project leader was Clare Saunders, a principal electronics engineer with the company. Clare's task was to pull all of the aspects of the project together using both her own skills and the different skills of the rest of the team.

The design team came up with a number of possibilities. It was finally decided that the unit would need to have the component parts shown below, a chassis to carry all of the components, and an outer shell. The team thought the layout shown below would make the best use of limited space.

Once the component parts and their relative positioning had been decided upon, the design for the chassis and casings could be considered. The overall size was determined by the size and layout of the components. The positioning also took into account the place of use, for example the shop counter. **Ergonomic** factors were also considered because the machine needed to be operated by people using the keyboard and card swipe.

More about ... ergonomics page 94.

The next thing to be determined was the way in which the components were to be fastened to the chassis. Were they to be clipped or screwed, permanent or semi-permanent fixings? Labour and component costings also had to be taken into consideration. The design team decided to use self-tapping screws, and clip fittings where possible in order to keep down assembly and material costs for each unit.

More about ... mechanical fasteners page 124.

The electronic parts of the unit were designed in-house and then sub-contracted to another company for manufacturing. This not only reduced the cost of retaining a specialised workforce, but it also gave the company more flexibility in that it did not need to carry specialised tools or stock.

◀ *Component parts of Cardmate 2.*

top view		underside view	
power supply	printer unit	paper roll	transformer to achieve required voltage
		modem / printer driver / beep	AC in / power 15 volts supply unit
		keyboard and display driver	microprocessor and memory
display	keyboard	card wipe / interface	microprocessor drives outside units e.g. printer and keyboard

Memory module contacts – module plugs in and contains unit identification

◀ *The layout of Cardmate 2.*

Manufacturing the chassis and casing

The chassis, casing and card swipe of the product were designed to be made of the same material – an **ABS plastic**, which is a **thermoplastic**. BEC, a company specialising in the production of plastics, was contracted to manufacture the components.

Using CAD/CAM to produce a mould

Drawings were generated at Racal Transcom using a **computer-aided design (CAD)** system. The design team discussed these and made minor modifications where necessary. The final design drawings were then sent to BEC. The CAD information was sent using a modem and a telephone line, and put directly onto the computer at BEC.

The design engineer at BEC checked the information and, knowing that the material to be used for the plastic mouldings was to be an ABS plastic, he adjusted the drawings to allow for the shrinkage of the material after moulding. At this point areas where the **sprues** were to occur on the moulding were also added to the drawings. From this information he was able to calculate the amount of raw material which was to go into each moulding.

> **You try it ...**
> Use CAD to create a drawing of a moulded plastic product.

> **More about ...** using computers in design and manufacturing page 103.

The information stored in the computer was enough to enable the production of a mould. The CAD information was then **downloaded** directly to a **CAD/CAM (computer-aided manufacture)** machine, which automatically produced a solid copy of the product in either copper or carbon. This product was transferred to an etching machine, which electrically etched the mould out of steel. This process can take up to four days. The etching produces a textured surface on the steel which can be reproduced on the actual product or, if a smooth surface is required, the mould needs to have the etching marks polished out.

The mould could now be checked for detail and transferred to the moulding presses. These are **injection units** and the company have a variety of machines ranging from a one-ton to a twenty-ton press. The mould for Racal Transcom Ltd had to be fitted into a ten ton press to give the material the required hardness and surface finish detail.

The injection moulding process

Injection moulding machines usually have the following components:

- a heater and injection unit for **plasticising** the thermoplastic while conveying it from the hopper to the mould;
- a locking unit for closing, clamping and opening the mould;
- a mould to receive, shape and cool the plastic;
- parts that are needed for the working and sequencing of the machine.

The feed hopper is loaded with the raw material beads. These are fed into the heating cylinder which melts the material. The heated contents are then forced into the closed mould by the plunger. The mould is cooled and then opened up to release the finished moulding. Sprue gates that are left on after moulding are broken off. The moulding is placed in a polythene bag to prevent it from being scratched. The finished mouldings are returned to the Racal Transcom factory ready for assembling.

> **More about ...** casting and moulding page 118.

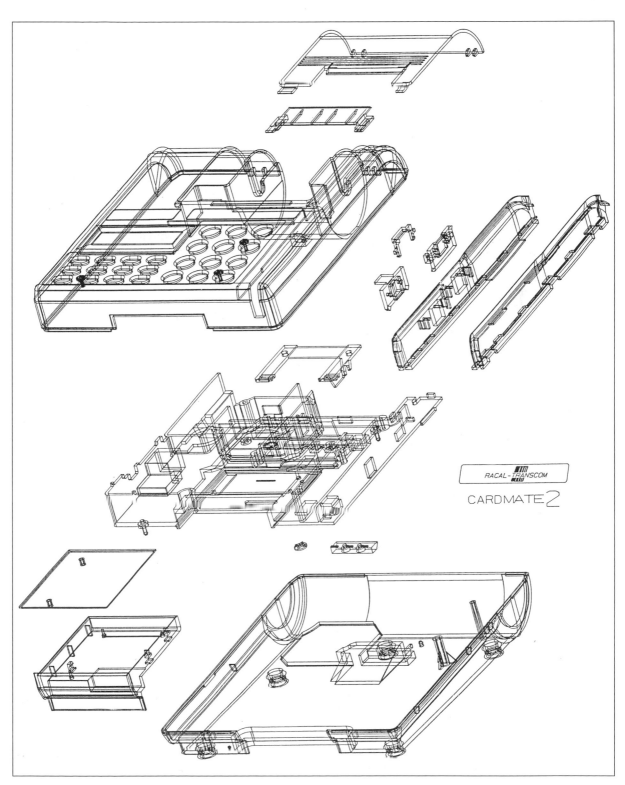

RACAL-TRANSCOM

CARDMATE 2

▲ *CAD drawing showing exploded view of plastic parts used in Cardmate 2.*

A simple plunger injection ▶
moulding machine.

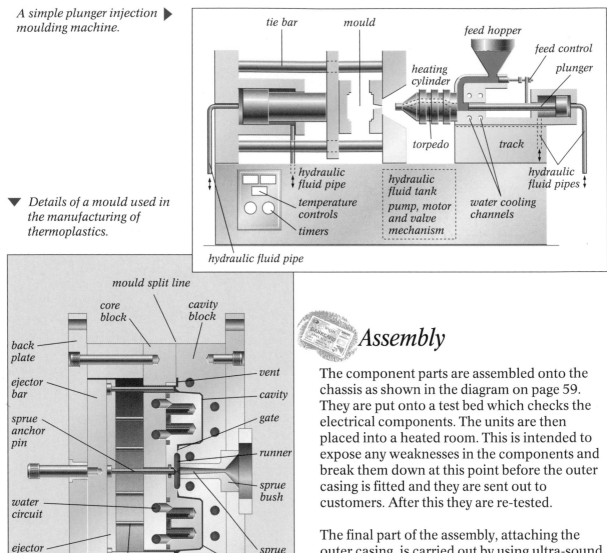

▼ Details of a mould used in
the manufacturing of
thermoplastics.

Assembly

The component parts are assembled onto the chassis as shown in the diagram on page 59. They are put onto a test bed which checks the electrical components. The units are then placed into a heated room. This is intended to expose any weaknesses in the components and break them down at this point before the outer casing is fitted and they are sent out to customers. After this they are re-tested.

The final part of the assembly, attaching the outer casing, is carried out by using ultra-sound. Ultra-sonic vibrations are set up in the materials which are fixed into a jig. The ultra-sound creates friction between the surfaces and thereby heats and melts the surfaces together. Joining the materials in this way prevents anyone tampering with the interior components and also acts as a security device.

A design fault became apparent at this point – the card swipe slot was also being melted and joined because it was narrow. It was necessary to rethink this component. The solution was to change the material used for this component and the ABS was replaced by polycarbonate which has a greater heat resistance.

You try it ...

Look at plastic modelling kits and see if you can see the sprues from the moulding. Why do you think they were made like this? If you look at a complex moulding, for example a telephone, can you identify where the sprues have been and why they were located at these points?

More about ... plastics page 114.

Installation and maintenance

The sales and marketing of Cardmate 2 are done mainly through the banks and finance houses. The company only deals directly with the retailers for the installation, maintenance and research and development of the machine.

On receipt of an order for the machine the company sends to the customer the machine, and installation and operating instructions. The customer is also supplied with a memory module which carries information about the siting of the machine and details of the customer. Once the customer has carried out the installation and typed in basic instructions, the module contacts the company using its modem to indicate that it is on-line and correctly installed. This information is received in the company's computer room from where the information is checked and the machine coded to allow it to operate at the site.

During use the machine makes regular diagnostic checks on itself and reports any faults and failings back to Racal Transcom via the modem. If, for instance, the machine fails to read a certain number of plastic cards it sends this information back to the company. From this information the company could decide if there was a need to replace the machine.

Replacement requires Racal Transcom sending another machine by post to the retailer and receiving the faulty machine via the same way.

On receipt of the faulty machine it is stripped of the outer casings, repaired and given a new outer casing, and sent out onto site again.

Summary

In this case study you have looked at:

- **a specialist IT company that focuses particularly on design and development of EFTPOS machines;**
- **how a brief for a new product is produced through consultation with different users;**
- **the importance of teamwork in developing a complex design;**
- **the use of CAD/CAM in manufacturing a mould for thermoplastic injection moulding;**
- **how a fault that appears at a manufacturing stage may be corrected by modifying the design.**

You will now be able to complete the tasks below which may form part or all of your coursework.

1 Form a design team to do the following.
 Look at the layout of components on an electrical appliance. Discuss the layout and how the designers have arrived at this solution. Would you change anything?
 Look at the surface texture of the material. Why is it finished in this way?
 How have ergonomics been considered in the design?
 Make a sketch of the product. Use colour to enhance your drawings.
 How is the product joined? Can you see any reasons why it is joined in this way?
 What materials have been used in the construction? Why?

More about ... ergonomics page 94.

2 Many materials are given extra strength by forming ribs and other shapes into the material. Use a vacuum-forming machine to create shapes in ABS plastic which would give the material extra strength that it does not possess as a flat sheet. Create a test rig which will enable you to carry out destructive tests. Record and compare results for various shapes.

More about ... formers page 119.

President Office Furniture

▲ *President logo.*

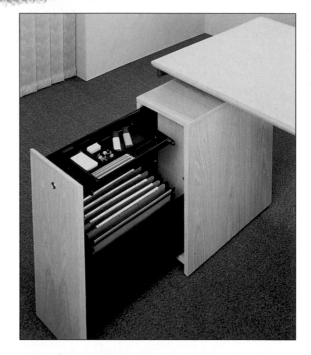

▲ *Skandinavisk Group logo.*

President Office Furniture is part of the Arenson Group plc which began as a one-person business hand-crafting wooden furniture. The group is now part of the Skandinavisk Group, one of the leading manufacturers of office furniture and associated products in Europe.

President has over 300 employees and an annual turnover of £25 million. It is a single-site manufacturer of office furniture. All the forming and fabrication of the wooden components of their furniture systems takes place on-site, with plastic and metal components supplied by outside companies to the company's design **specification**. The manufacturing operation is sufficiently flexible and responsive to allow products to be made to order – no products are kept in stock. Most sales are via dealers to larger organisations like multi-national corporations and government departments.

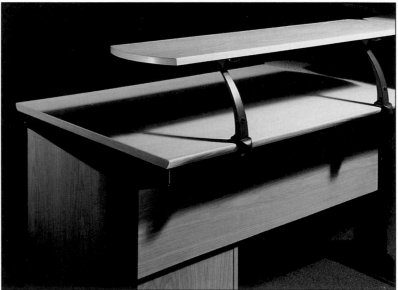

▲ ◄ *Three key requirements for office furniture systems are work surfaces, storage and ways of defining work spaces, for example through screens. These products are from President's* ◄ *Aria range.*

Leading the market

President's management decided to try to actively lead the office furniture **market** in design rather than merely reacting to emerging trends. Research had identified several issues affecting the market. The experience of the sales team indicated that some parts of President's existing product ranges addressed these issues, but no one product range covered all of them.

President wanted to produce a product that reflected these market trends in Europe. The design wasn't to be constrained by current production technologies. To help them develop this new range, the in-house design team decided to engage FM Design, a company with product design experience in the European market.

Roger Carr of FM Design explains:

'Our primary function was to question everything, to turn over the rules in a structured way, to design a product for four to five years ahead, effectively just over the perceived horizon.'

The Kyo research and development project had begun.

◄ *Kyo logo.*

▼ *Products from the Kyo range.*

Kyo

You try it ...

What do you think makes a good design for office furniture? Is the furniture in your school library or office well-designed?

Using market research findings

The Kyo range was developed after extensive **market research** in the UK, continental Europe and the USA. President also used feedback from the existing customer base of users, specifiers and focus groups of related professionals. This information provided a clear understanding of what the market really wanted.

The main issues identified were:

- furniture systems need to be more flexible in use to match changing work and employment patterns;
- they need to incorporate increased servicing (connections to electricity power points, computer networks, telephone lines etc.);
- the number of items of furniture should be minimised – for example, by a single piece of furniture having more than one use or function.

You try it ...
Set up some market research to find out about teenagers' attitudes, likes, dislikes and needs in relation to furniture design.

More about ... market research page 97.

Changes in work and employment patterns

Large organisations all over the world face problems of a rapidly reducing workforce because of economic and technological factors. In the past organisations used rectangular-shaped office furniture to define the territory and status of different workers; with changes to a 'flatter', team-based approach to management this is no longer appropriate or

helpful. The growth of information technology and the flexibility it brings means that routine work can now take place away from the office. Ideas like job sharing also challenge commonly held views of what resources will efficiently support employees.

The design of most office furniture determines how it can be used. Other product ranges from President Office Furniture still reflect this. The planning page opposite shows that several functions can be accommodated using combinations of units from the Aria range. The problem is that these are heavy pieces of furniture which are difficult to move and re-configure. Generally they are rarely moved.

Increased servicing needs

The growth of information technology in offices has vastly increased servicing needs of each workstation or desk. For example, at one time a worker may need a simple flat surface to write on, and at another time access to computing facilities and on-line data channels. The computer could be a desk-top PC or a lap-top, each one requiring power, access to networking and printing facilities.

▼ *Information technology places great demands on services.*

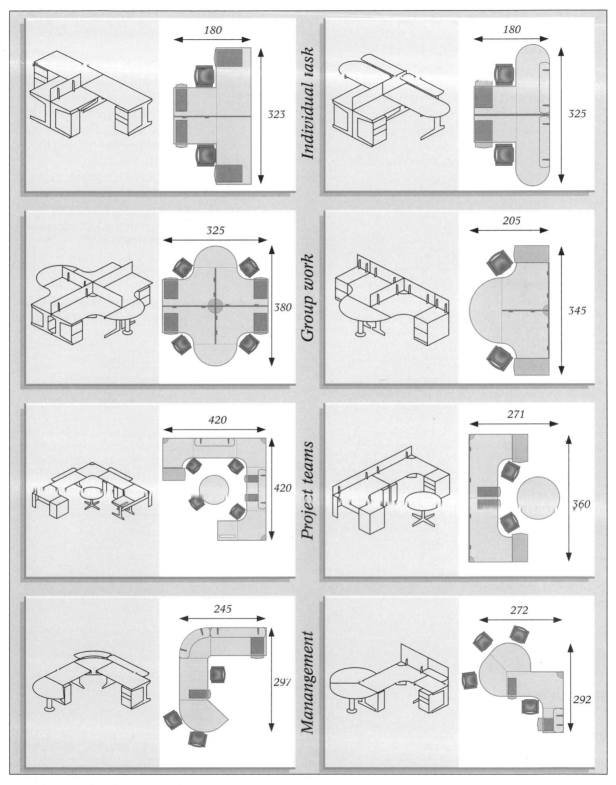

▲ *Planning page for Aria product range.*

Minimising office furniture

Office managers require only the furniture that is absolutely necessary. Companies are switching to offices where space and resources are shared between several employees, sometimes called 'hot-desking'.

> **You try it ...**
>
> What do you think a modern school desk should look like? How does your own working space at home meet your needs?

The Kyo design in detail

Kyo is designed to allow the user to decide what layout they want at any given time. It is a 'loose-fit' system, enabling a greater variation in planning workspace options at either a macro (organisational) or a micro (individual) level. Kyo supports ways of working where tasks, responsibilities and needs can change, from moment to moment, from project to project and from stage to stage in the development of a company. Storage and division of space are simplified by a set of functional elements that can be moved, adapted for change of use or combined with other elements.

Although there are fewer basic elements in the Kyo range, it can provide many different shapes or layout **configurations**. The gas-lift height-adjustment system adds to the range's versatility. For example, a meeting table can double as a computer desktop; by adjusting the height, it can be used for presentations, or by people standing (a practice more common in continental European countries).

Ease of mobility is a key design idea in the Kyo range. The ability to move and reposition the furniture quickly as the need arises is more efficient than having a greater number of dedicated furniture elements.

A flexible, non-permanent method of installation provides divisions that are easy to place where they are needed and to remove

▼ *The full Kyo range.*

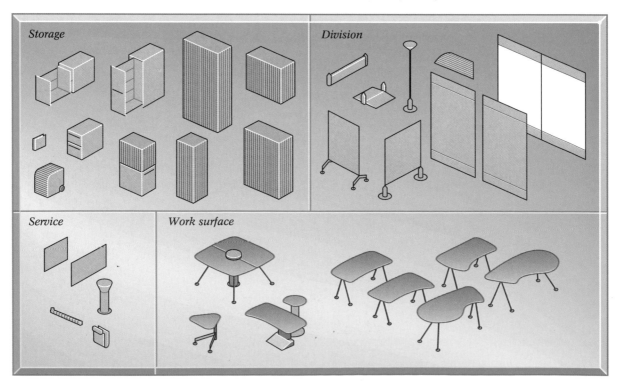

Storage

Division

Service

Work surface

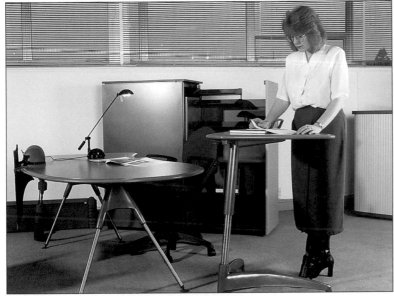

Kyo Petal table in use.

when necessary. The screens can be joined together at any angle to define an office space or create a personalised work area. There is a need in any office or study area for quiet or acoustic privacy. Because they are not fixed the 'walls' are easy to rearrange or take way altogether.

Individual users of Kyo items have a greater degree of control over their working environment. The height and angle of work spaces, the position of screens and the precise location of a storage system are simply altered to reflect individual preferences and **ergonomic** requirements. For example, electric remote control allows the height of the Arc workstation to be adjusted even when it is supporting heavy office equipment.

Kyo provides different servicing options on each desk or workstation. The concept of multi-level servicing means that various capabilities can be easily attached or drawn up to the work surface as required.

▲ *The gas-lift system in close-up.*

The screening system. ▶

◀ *The Arc workstation.*

▼ *Servicing the Kyo range of desks. The service point clips onto the table top at any position.*

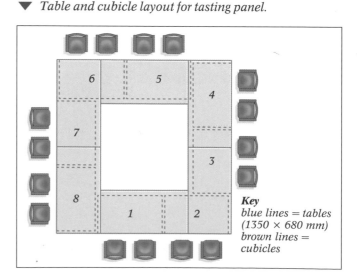

You try it ...

The marketing department of a large multi-national food manufacturer is setting up a programme of mobile regional food tasting panels which will meet in various locations, mostly small halls. In the interests of fair testing members of the panel need to be separated from one another when they are tasting the food and forming their opinions or answering questionnaires. Afterwards they come together to talk as a group about the products they have been tasting.

The layout of the collapsible tables and cubicles is shown. The chairs are adjustable for height. Your task is to produce designs for a method of individual but linked screening to provide individual cubicles for tasters to sit in during the tasting programme. The cubicles have to be easily dismantled by the members of the panel when the group discussion session begins. You also have to provide a source of lighting for each cubicle to ensure standard lighting conditions during the tasting. Present your ideas in the form of dimensioned sketches and diagrams. Show clearly how the panels join together and how the light fittings are attached.

▼ *Table and cubicle layout for tasting panel.*

Key
blue lines = tables (1350 × 680 mm)
brown lines = cubicles

From brief to prototype

Generally, designing consumer-based products involves well-detailed design briefs and tight specifications. There is usually a concentration on reducing costs and improving profitability while providing a product that consumers want or can be persuaded to buy. Discussion may be limited to formal presentations and informal progress reports.

The brief for Kyo was much more *open* in terms of price areas, target customers and manufacturing constraints. Roger Carr of FM Design comments:

'The information we started off with was gradually refined over a series of stages until in time it became the basis of the technical specification. Discussion is an essential part of any design development – in some cases it can account for 60 per cent of the time we spend on a project. In turn FM Design has its own aspirations; we are in the business of promoting a design culture – a desire to change things for the better.'

You try it ...

In a group of three, consider the needs of a range of users of an office chair. Write an open design brief for the chair.

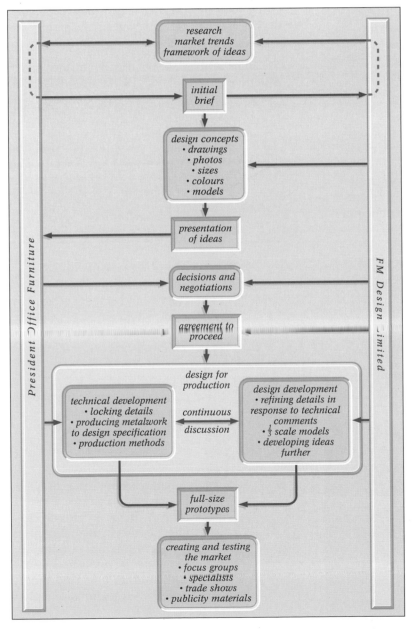

◀ *The roles of President and FM Design in developing the Kyo product range.*

Looking at past designs and present needs

Roger explains what FM Design's product research and analysis had found out:

'The traditional model of a furniture system is something that fits together, connects or interconnects in all sorts of ways. It is a sort of cumbersome Meccano™ or LEGO™ kit with holes and fittings all over the place to attach things to. Designers were actually trying to design and build in facilities to match all future possibilities but they were building in over-complex and, in some situations, redundant features. What happened when there was a change of user or a piece of new technology equipment was introduced?'

FM Design did what was essentially a de-construction job. The standard office desk used to be aimed at one user doing essentially one job function. However, the modern office environment needs desks with conveniently placed storage where people can sit and work individually, but also where a group of people can sit around and discuss ideas.

The growth of heavy computer systems and telecommunications equipment presented a further series of design challenges. Another key design factor was the need to meet performance standards and health and safety directives that dictate how people should use computers in the workplace.

From these factors, FM Design needed to specify design parameters in terms of mobility, space division, storage space, services. They came up with the idea of a basic shape that could be changed and adapted easily by the addition of specific modules.

You try it ...

List the key design features of the Kyo concept. Use it to evaluate an existing office furniture system, highlighting similarities and differences.

Choose one component or product, such as a desk, to review and analyse in more detail. Use sketches or diagrams to show what you think are the key design features of the product you are looking at.

▲ *A desk from the 1970s.*

Thinking up new ideas

The creative bit was the stage Roger and his team were waiting for:

'Once we had stripped the ideas down to the bare essentials, we set to and had a bit of fun! Design is only a headache when you've got a blank piece of paper. We had an exciting brief, we knew the limitations.'

When working in a group designers don't agree all the time. At Roger's company the idea of the 'vocal challenge' is used. Any member of the group can verbally disagree with another but must offer positive suggestions in reply.

You try it ...
From your list of key design features of the Kyo concept, choose what you think are the two most important features. Then discuss your choices with others in your group. Use the technique of 'vocal challenge' to agree as a group on the two main design features.

Checking manufacturability at an early stage

An essential part of the design development process involved looking at the 'tooling' required to achieve certain end results. Several visits were made to the President manufacturing site to see the existing production techniques. It also gave the opportunity to talk through early ideas with expert production staff, which would avoid costly mistakes later.

Presenting the ideas – prototype models

Presenting design ideas can take many forms. One of the key tools in the design of Kyo proved to be scale models of the items, made by FM Modelmakers, a specialist 'model shop' on the same site as FM Design. This meant that models of designs could be produced very quickly, enabling the designer to see any problems with the design almost immediately.

The **prototype** models eventually produced were used as the final test of the design concept. The reaction of experts attending specialist furniture trade shows helped to indicate reaction to, and support for, the idea. It also provided a measure of the potential volume of the market.

More about ... using models page 108.

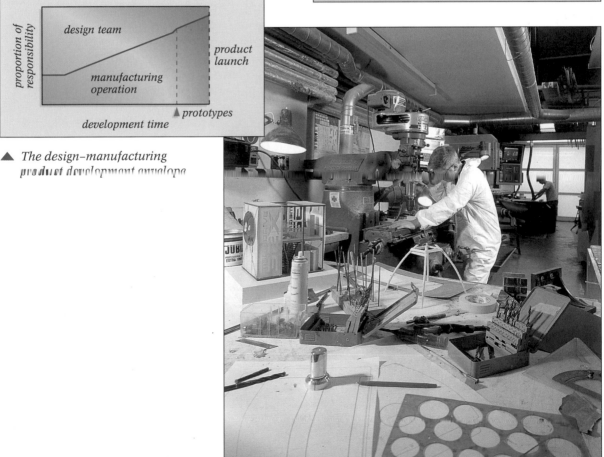

▲ *The design–manufacturing product development envelope.*

The model shop at FM Design. ▶

Marketing Kyo

All the literature and promotional material for Kyo was put together as a collaboration between the sales and marketing departments at President and a graphic design company called The Design Clinic. The various materials reflect the concepts behind the range. The front cover features repeated Kyo logos linking together in a variety of ways, just like the product itself.

▲ *The brochure layout showing links to advertising material.*

▲ *A selection from the A4 poster campaign in trade journals.*

Setting quality indicators for manufacture

Quality has become a key word in all successful manufacturing companies. **Quality indicators** – written statements in a specification that set the acceptable limits for a component or product – are an essential part of a **quality assurance** system.

At President, **quality control** starts at goods inwards. All suppliers know that any item entering the factory is inspected for quality before it is passed into production stock. Any items which are not up to the required standard are returned to the supplier.

One aspect President are actively assessing and monitoring is the **environmental impact** of the manufacturing operation, the products and the components that go into the products. For example, all the chipboard used in the products is supplied from farmed forest plantations. The production of chipboard involves the use of formaldehyde, which can be a hazardous substance in certain situations. President specify chipboard that contains low amounts of this chemical.

▼ *President's environmental logo.*

You try it ...

How would you check the quality of a stock length of softwood? Would the quality checks differ for hardwoods and veneers? Produce a list of quality indicators you would use to select wood-based materials for a piece of domestic furniture.

More about ... quality page 98.

Preparing the materials

Cutting the wood panels roughly to size

The wood panels, which are either chipboard or medium density fibreboard (MDF), arrive in 5 tonne packages measuring 5.5 metres by 2.5 metres. The whole package is automatically sawn into stock lengths and widths in one operation using a bank of powered sawing machines. The length is cut using circular rip saw blades, the width using circular cross-cut saws.

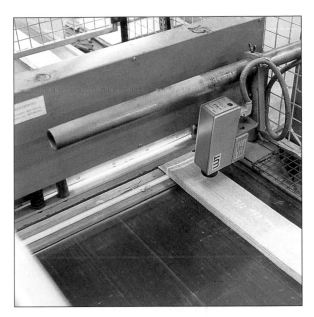

▲ *The photo-electric cell detector in operation.*

You try it ...

1 Compare the structure of chipboard with medium density fibreboard (MDF). Using actual products as examples, explain how the structure of the two materials affects the way they can be fabricated and formed.

2 Explain the principles behind how a saw cuts a piece of wood. What are the similarities and differences between rip saws and cross-cut saws?

More about ... wood composites page 113.
More about ... wasting methods page 120.

Preparing the veneers

At the same time the wood veneers or decorative plastic **laminates** are prepared. Computer-based systems and electronic controls are used to monitor the quality of these thin sections of material. For example, defects in wood veneers are detected using a photo-electric cell system. Once the length of veneer has passed electronic and visual inspection, it is automatically guillotined to the appropriate length.

The width of wood veneers is always limited by the way they are produced from the original sawn tree-trunk. To get the width needed to cover a table or desktop panel, they are jointed using fibreglass thread with a hot melt adhesive.

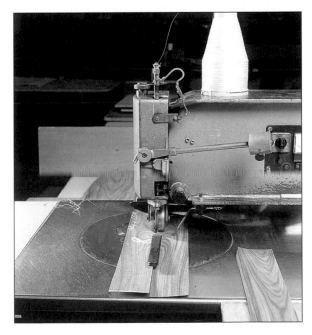

▲ *The veneer jointing technique.*

The plastic laminate sheets (melamine) are cut to size using a computer-controlled machine. A scoring cut is made to a depth of one millimetre before the final cut is made. This prevents the brittle plastic from chipping when it is cut and shaped.

You try it ...
Research and report on the methods used to produce hardwood veneers.

More about ... wood composites page 113.

Applying the veneer

The rough-cut wood panels pass on to one of two panel lines where the veneers or laminates are fixed in place using a combination of adhesive, heat and pressure. Several panels are veneered at the same time to reduce costs and speed up production. The glue is evenly spread over the panel using knife edge rollers on a lay-up table where the veneers are fed onto the board automatically. The curing temperature for the adhesive is 125 °C and the process takes about 40 seconds.

You try it ...
Investigate the process of laminating thin decorative veneers. Try out the process using a small section of plywood or MDF as your base material. You could produce several small samples using a range of adhesives. You could also apply different weights during the pressing stage to see what effect that has on the finished product. What other variables could you change? Remember that you need to ensure that you are doing a fair test, for instance the sample boards should all be the same size. What other variables need to be fixed?

Produce a simple line flow chart to describe the method of veneering you used. How will you judge the effectiveness of the different variables on the finished veneered sample?

More about ... adhesives
page 127.

Cutting the panels to size

The panels are carried forward on air flotation tables which supply small jets of air to lift the panel. This not only protects the veneer but also allows the heavy panels to be moved more easily.

President Office Furniture have installed a computer-controlled routing machine to produce large panels and table tops. It produces the large complicated curved shapes and the necessary fixing holes in one complete pass. The machine can be set up to produce a new shape in a very short time because all the machining data is held in the machine's central microprocessor unit. A safety feature of the machine is that it is guarded by infra-red beams and opto-reflectors rather than conventional high impact plastic or metal guards. Once a beam is 'broken' a danger signal is sent to the machine's processing unit. All power to the machine is immediately switched off and the cutters automatically retract into a fail-safe position.

▼ *Computer-controlled routing machine: (a) the microprocessor panel; (b) the overall machine.*

(b)

(a)

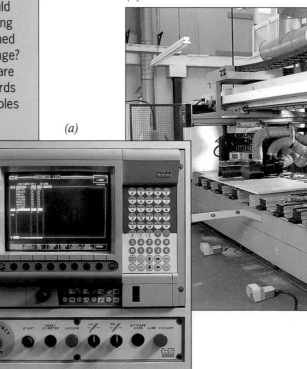

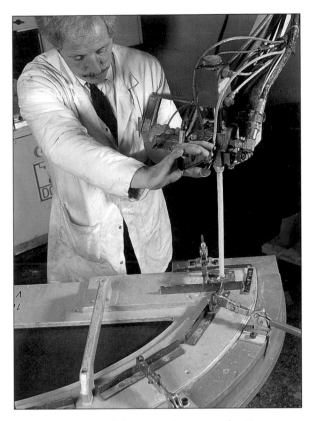

▲ *Injection moulding the edges on a plastic laminate panel.*

Applying edging

The panels are finished using edge laminates or moulded synthetic plastic materials such as polyurethane. The edge laminates provide a two-dimensional effect whereas the moulded edges are three-dimensional in character.

The polyurethane edge is moulded using an injection technique and specially shaped latex rubber formers. The latex rubber is so flexible that it is even possible to simulate wood grain on the finished moulding.

More about ... plastics page 114; injection moulding page 118.

Surface finishing

The veneered surfaced boards are passed through a series of operations in readiness for the surface finishing process. If the veneers are to be stained or dyed, the edges are sprayed first and then the panel faces. The thickness of the veneer at this stage is 0.6 mm – after the finishing process it is in the region of 0.4 mm.

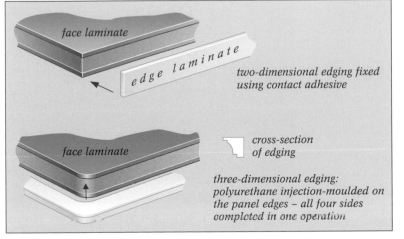

face laminate

edge laminate

two-dimensional edging fixed using contact adhesive

face laminate

cross-section of edging

three-dimensional edging: polyurethane injection-moulded on the panel edges – all four sides completed in one operation

▲ *Two-dimensional and three-dimensional edging.*

The surface finishing line for panels.

Stage	Process
1 Brush unit	The panel passes through a brush unit to remove the dust caused during manufacture.
2 Barrier coat	A barrier coat is applied to the veneer to avoid a subsequent loss of colour; for example, American White Oak veneer loses its clear white colour when finishing lacquer is applied to it.
3 Dryer	The barrier coat is dried using infra-red heat.
4 First base coat	First base coat is applied – a solvent-free acrylic lacquer at 0.7 g per 300 mm square. The thinner the coat, the finer the finish.
5 UV curing unit	Lacquer cured by ultra-violet (UV).
6 Second base coat	Second base coat applied.
7 UV curing unit	Base coat cured by UV.
8 Sanding	Nibbing down – abrasive sanding machines remove minor surface irregularities.
9 Brush unit	Brush unit removes abrasive dust.
10 Stain application	Further stain applied.
11 Dryer	The stain is dried using infra-red heat.
12 Top coat	Top coat – acrylic lacquer applied at 0.5 g per 300 mm square.

Assembly and packing

From the finishing line the panels pass onto the assembly area where all locking cams, dowels, catches, locks, hinges and other fittings are put in place. All the components needed for one complete product pack including assembly instructions are brought together to create the product flat pack which the customer receives. The complete package is wrapped in protective material and banded up using plastic strips. The finished product pack passes into the distribution warehouse.

Flat packs and dimensional co-ordination

There has been a revolution in the areas of furnishing and building with the introduction of flat-pack self-assembly furniture. President Office Furniture supply their larger product items such as desks and tables in this form.

▲ *Flat packs at President Office Furniture.*

This advance has been made possible not only by improved fastening technology but also by **dimensional co-ordination**, a design system which uses standard **anthropometric data**. Kitchen design companies, for example, almost always adopt a modular approach to their design work unless it is a made-to-measure one off installation.

You try it ...

Flat pack systems have costs and benefits for both manufacturers and consumers. Choosing examples from the furniture industry, discuss the advantages and disadvantages from:

- the manufacturer's and distributor's point of view,
- the consumer's position.

More about ... dimensional co-ordination page 106.

Summary

In this case study you have looked at:

- **teamwork between design consultants and a manufacturing company;**
- **developing an innovative product by analysing past products and by researching present user needs and emerging market trends;**
- **using models to present and test ideas, as prototypes, and as marketing tools;**
- **setting quality indicators for manufacture,**

and using computer-controlled equipment to check that materials meet them;
- **preparation methods used with wood-based materials – sawing, veneering, routing, edging, surface finishing;**
- **using CNC machines in manufacture, including automatic safety features;**
- **flat pack furniture products and dimensional co-ordination.**

You will now be able to complete the tasks below which may form part or all of your coursework.

1 Using a systems electronic kit, model how you think the automatic machine for detecting defects in the veneers operates (see page 75). Record your ideas in the form of a block or circuit diagram. You could use a light dependent resistor to simulate the 'electric eye'. Develop your solution further so that it incorporates the guillotine that cuts the veneers to length. You can use any suitable output device to simulate when the guillotine is operating. What safety precautions do you need to put in place to protect the people using your machine?

2 Think about the different tasks and activities that you do and the ways in which you do your school work either at home or in a classroom. List all the activities, grouping similar ones together. Compare your list with at least two other members in your group, using the technique of vocal challenge (see page 72). Produce a new list that you all agree on. Working on your own, design an individual working space to reflect the variety of tasks and activities that you have to do.

Naim Audio Limited

Naim Audio Limited, based in Salisbury, Wiltshire, produces very high quality audio equipment for hi-fi enthusiasts and people who want sound quality which is close to listening to a live performance.

The company's products, which are designed primarily for the home market, with some studio applications, span the whole hi-fi system chain. All products are designed, developed, assembled, tested and finished in-house. It is company policy not to sub-contract anything above the **piece part** or component stage of any process.

In all of the design work the company follows the basic shape and colour of its existing range, which enables customers to match new units with previous purchases. New products are designed so that they are usually compatible with older equipment, which enables customers to build up systems over a period of years. Existing customers can, at a cost, have their systems upgraded as improved components or assembly techniques become available.

The range includes three CD players, three FM tuners, a pick-up arm, four pre-amps, power supplies, an integrated amplifier, five power **amplifiers**, two electronic crossovers and three models of loudspeakers. These can be combined to form a system of the very highest quality. Seventy specialist shops in the UK are supplied direct.

History of Naim

The company was founded by Julian Vereker in 1969. The first product was a sound-to-light unit which was capable of switching 30 kW of lighting on and off in time to music. The unit produced enough light to illuminate an entire film set and was hired out to other companies for use in film production.

◀ *Naim product range.*

▲ *One of the original mixer desks designed and made by Julian Vereker.*

Julian was passionately interested in music. He made recordings of friends' live performances at home but was unhappy with the recordings. He found it difficult to tell which instruments were being played.

He tried to solve the problem by building a mixer; this would enable him to separate the individual sound inputs and adjust the sound levels to balance the recording, but it did not lead to any great improvement in the final recordings. (However, the design of the mixer

was so good that more were produced and sold to the BBC and individual recording studios.) He designed and built a speaker, which helped a little. He added a commercially-produced amplifier, which was thought to be of high quality at the time, to the system, but this actually made things worse. So he designed and made his own.

In 1974 Julian met Ivor Tiefenbrum, who designed and made his own turntables. They both thought that the units receiving the signals were the most important and the speakers the least important when it came to setting up a hi-fi system. (This was contrary to what was generally believed at that time, but hi-fi enthusiasts now universally accept this view.)

Julian and Ivor decided to work together to promote their products throughout the world. As the chart on page 82 shows, the company was successful and grew throughout the 1970s and 1980s. Naim now employs over 80 people and has an annual turnover of £5 000 000.

▼ *Configuration of equipment.*

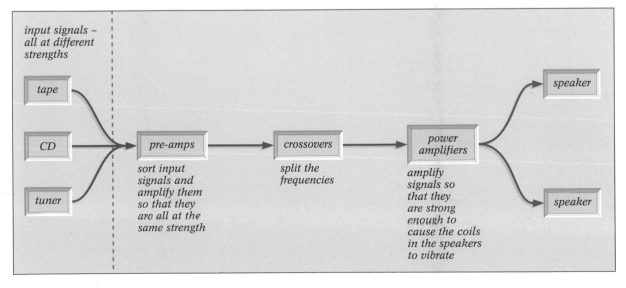

Company development.

1969	Company founded by Julian Vereker, run from basement of house in Salisbury Sound-to-light unit produced
1970	Mixer and speakers developed and produced
1971	First Naim power amplifier sold Amplifiers and mixers sold to friends, acquaintances and a few recording studios
1973	Contract to supply Capital Radio (independent station in London) with 24 loudspeakers Naim Audio Limited formed
1974	Company moves to sixteenth-century shop in Salisbury city centre Julian Vereker and Ivor Tiefenbrum promote their products throughout world
1980	Naim amplifiers and Tiefenbrum turntables very successful Nine Naim staff moved to factory with 1022 m² floor area Product range extended to include FM tuner; rest of range improved Exports to 26 countries, including USA, Canada, Japan and most of Europe
1985	Factory extended to 1858 m² Company won Queen's Award for Export Achievement
1986	Naim Audio North America Inc. opened in Chicago, USA, with warehouse, office and demonstration facilities
1994	Substantial expansion programme enlarged UK research and development, factory and demonstration facilities to 3159 m²

> **You try it ...**
>
> What would you look for in a good hi-fi system?

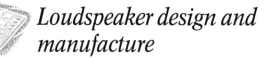

Loudspeaker design and manufacture

Naim make three models of loudspeaker, all of which use a common design principle.

Speaker design at Naim

The main scientific principle used in general loudspeaker design is electromagnetism. A current in a magnetic field experiences a force at right angles to the direction of current flow and magnetic field. In a speaker, the electrical signal from the amplifier passes through a coil of wire which is surrounded by a strong magnetic field. The coil is attached to a cone which vibrates at the same frequency as the signal passing through the coil. The vibration produces sound waves in the surrounding air. The higher frequencies are sent to the tweeter speaker and the lower frequencies are sent to the bass speaker.

As well as the sound waves which are directed forwards by the cone, there are some which are directed backwards. These are 'out of phase' with the waves at the front and so they need to be 'baffled' to prevent them causing amplitude cancellation. In the past, large boxes were used to absorb the sound waves produced at the back of the speaker. A later development was to put fibres into the box to deaden the sound. Naim

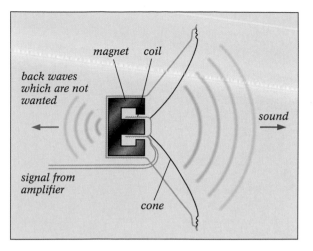

▲ *Sound waves in a speaker.*

have overcome this problem by 'fooling' the bass speaker. This is achieved by adding a second 'expansion' box connected to the main box by a gasket and an acoustic resistance membrane.

The acoustic resistance membrane is made up of strips of plastic (polythene) bolted together. Each strip of polythene has tiny ribs on it. The ribs prevent the strips of polythene from sticking together and also allow the air to pass through the membrane into the lower box. The combination of the bass expansion box and the acoustic resistance membrane fools the bass driver in a way which mimics the effect when the driver is put in a box of much larger dimensions.

In order to reduce vibration between the speaker boxes, they are set up on a metal frame and mounted on pinpoint fixings; these are adjustable in height which enable the speaker to be located accurately on the floor.

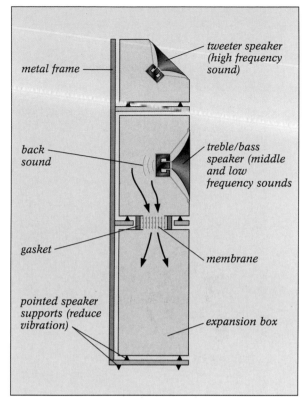

▲ *Layout of Naim speaker boxes.*

▼ *Construction of membrane.*

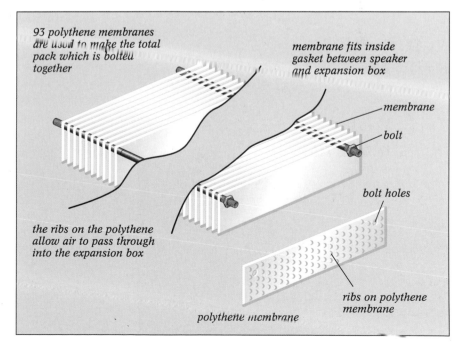

▲ *The rear of the speakers mounted on frame.*

▼ *Speaker parts.*

You try it ...

1 Investigate loudspeaker characteristics by monitoring sound levels at different distances and/or angles from a speaker cabinet. (The science department may be able to help here.)

2 Take an old loudspeaker cabinet apart and look at the different speakers and the materials used.

More about ... materials page 111.

Manufacturing and testing the speaker units

The component parts for the speakers are manufactured by another company; the parts are then assembled using a variety of adhesives at Naim Audio Limited. One of the main adhesives used is of an epoxy type. This type was chosen because it will form a strong bond between dissimilar materials and also withstand the continual vibrations. Other adhesives used are acrylic and cyanoacrylate. All of the adhesives used produce fumes and so gluing takes place inside a fume cupboard in order to protect the operator.

The speaker drive units are tested and their output at different frequencies is plotted on a graph. Drivers producing the same output are paired and kept together from this point onwards. This ensures that there is no mismatch between the speakers.

You try it ...

Cut a selection of materials to a set size and, using different adhesives, glue different materials together and test them to see which adhesives are best for particular materials. You can devise your own test rigs for this. Try using a variety of recording methods when compiling your results.

More about ... adhesives page 127.

▲ *Matched pairs of speakers in the stores.*

Speaker assembly

The speaker boxes are made using MDF (medium density fibreboard). This material was chosen for the following reasons:

- it has a very flat finish and will accept veneers and paints easily;
- it does not move with changes in the humidity of the air;
- it can easily be machined;
- it is compact enough to retain screws permanently;
- it is of a suitable weight for the job and does not easily vibrate.

The speaker boxes are veneered; these are manufactured in Denmark as this was the only place where a company could be found to match the veneers used. The boxes are matched in pairs so that both have the same wood grain lines running through them at the same point. They are then painted black to match the rest of the company's products and to fit in with the company's image.

The speakers and speaker boxes are assembled. A test is run to see if any further distortion in sound quality occurs and that they still match. The completed speakers are transferred to the packing area ready for dispatch.

All leads used for the speakers are marked with arrows to show the direction in which the cable was manufactured because this affects the sound quality. All cables are therefore made to fit in one direction only.

> **You try it ...**
> Find out ways of joining MDF as a box structure and consider which would be the most appropriate method to use for attaching veneers on its surfaces.

> **More about ...** wood composites page 113.

 *Production*

The production department covers a number of areas: **PCB** manufacture, casings, main assembly and wiring, speakers, testing, knobs and fascias, and packaging. One of the largest of these areas is PCB manufacture.

Stock control systems

The production department deals with small batch numbers. The maximum number of any unit being manufactured at a time is 21. Components used for manufacturing are ordered or reproduced as they are required. A ticket follows each unit through production and the initials of the people at each operation are filled in at every stage. This system allows the production department to maintain a high quality of work and to be able to back-check on any unsatisfactory work quality.

> **More about ...** quality page 98.

The company has a demand-led manufacturing system which keeps the amount of stock carried to a minimum. This system is known as a 'Kanban' system and is a 'lean manufacturing' method from Japan. For example, demand for PCBs triggers an immediate response by setting up a replenish system. The diagram shows how it works.

▼ *The stock control system.*

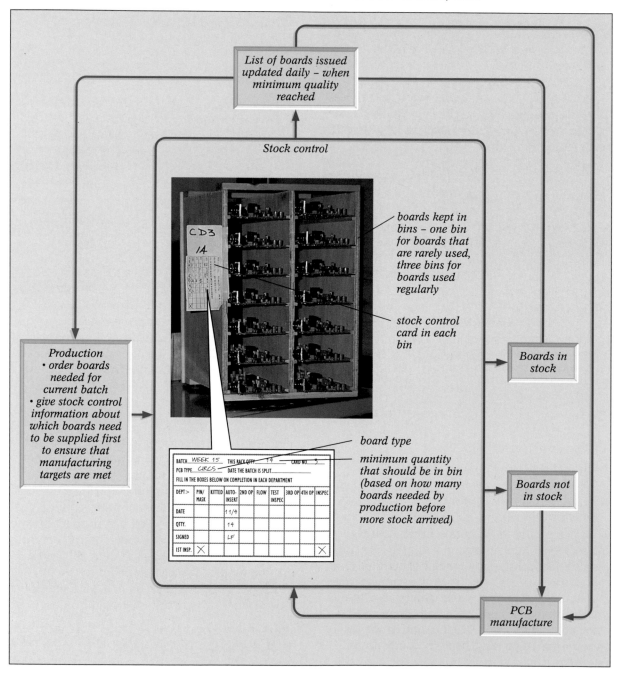

List of boards issued updated daily – when minimum quality reached

Stock control

CD3 1A

boards kept in bins – one bin for boards that are rarely used, three bins for boards used regularly

stock control card in each bin

Production
• order boards needed for current batch
• give stock control information about which boards need to be supplied first to ensure that manufacturing targets are met

Boards in stock

board type

minimum quantity that should be in bin (based on how many boards needed by production before more stock arrived)

Boards not in stock

PCB manufacture

| BATCH WEEK 15 THIS RACK QTY. 14 CARD NO. 5 |
| PCB TYPE CIRCS DATE THE BATCH IS SPLIT |
| FILL IN THE BOXES BELOW ON COMPLETION IN EACH DEPARTMENT |

DEPT>	PIN/ MASK	KITTED	AUTO-INSERT	2ND OP	FLOW	TEST INSPEC	3RD OP	4TH OP	INSPEC
DATE			11/4						
QTTY.			14						
SIGNED			LF						
1ST INSP.	X								X

PCB manufacture

The PCBs are designed, using **CAD**, to the company specifications at Naim but are manufactured to order by other companies.

> **More about ...** CAD page 103.

They are manufactured from fibreglass bonded by **epoxy resin**. The fibre mats are laid down in sheets sized 2 metres by 1 metre and epoxy resins are rolled into them. The sheets are compressed using a press and heat; this process 'cures' the board, hardens it and allows it to be handled immediately. The sheets are cut to the required shape and size.

Although it is more expensive than the paper-bonded boards that are frequently used, this type of construction was selected because it results in a higher heat resistance than paper-bonded boards. This is needed because certain areas of the board (hot spots) can reach 120 °C and overall operating temperatures of 70 °C are normal. Another factor is that the epoxy resin board has a high strength factor and therefore is difficult to break, which is an important consideration when manufacturing sound equipment which will be subject to many vibrations. Another consideration was that paper-bonded boards can suffer from mould in countries of high humidity, whereas fibreglass/epoxy resin boards resist mould attack.

Copper sheet which is up to 70 microns thick is bonded onto the boards using an epoxy resin and high pressure and temperature. The CAD artwork is used as the layout for an ultra-violet sensitive image which is exposed onto the board. The portions exposed to the ultra-violet light in this process will resist etching fluids. The copper which is not required for the circuit is etched away using iron (III) chloride, which leaves the circuit layout in copper on the board. This is then plated with a tin-lead compound. Boards can be made to be either single or double sided.

A **computer numerically controlled (CNC)** machine is used to drill holes in the board, using computer data supplied by the company. Some holes are 'plated through' to give electronic continuity to the other side of the board. **Jig** location holes are also drilled into the board so that it can be precisely positioned at all points in production. These are normally put on an outside edge which can be cut away once production is completed.

> **More about ...** jigs page 121.

The tinned copper of the board is protected by silk-screen printing with a green epoxy-based solder-resistant material on all parts of the copper except where soldered joints are required in the assembly. The PCBs are packed and sent to Naim Audio Limited and placed in the stores ready for use.

Computer-controlled assembly of components onto PCBs

The PCB production line is a mixture of automated processes and some hand assembly work. The boards are placed onto a jig in a machine which fixes the majority of components automatically.

▼ *PCB assembly machine showing reels of components on the left and cartridges of components on the right of the picture.*

Vertically fitting components are fed in from the right and horizontally fitting components are fed in from the left. Integrated circuits are fed in from a centrally mounted mechanism. The components which are used most are on reels and the least used components are stored in cartridges. This is because a greater number of a given component can be carried and made available from a reel, which can be quickly and easily replaced. Cartridges, by contrast, only carry a small number of a component type. Using these in large quantities would require frequent reloading and therefore stopping and delaying production. Once the components have been fixed on one board, the machine allows the operator to change the layout so that components can be fixed on the next board in the sequence.

A light is shone through the PCB and picked up by a camera located below the turntable. The image received by the camera is checked against a computer program for the correct alignment and location of the holes. The machine is given the information from the computer to select the correct components and place them into the correct holes. The surplus wire on the

▼ *PCB assembly machine layout. The computer controls the component types, positions the board and checks the hole locations by using the camera. The monitor shows the board positions as seen by the camera.*

components is cut off and the wire tails of the components are bent over at the correct angle and direction. This avoids any electrical shorting occurring between circuits.

Hand assembly

The part-finished boards are placed in bins on trolleys. The trolleys are taken to the hand assembly section where larger components, which cannot be handled by the automatic process, are fitted to the boards.

Soldering components onto boards

The next stage is to solder all the components onto the boards. This is done by a machine which applies flux to the areas requiring soldering and, using a lead/tin based solder, solders all the components onto the board.

The boards are passed over a sprayed flux which adheres to the bare copper parts. It is then passed over a heater which dries the flux and pre-heats the board ready for soldering. The pre-heating reduces the **thermal shock** on the board. The board passes over a wave of solder where the fluxed parts receive the solder. The operation is now complete.

After this, any components which still need to be fitted are added to the board. Components may have been left off up to this point because they could not stand up to the temperatures used or because they were too large to be accepted by the machines. The boards are sent to the testing area at this point.

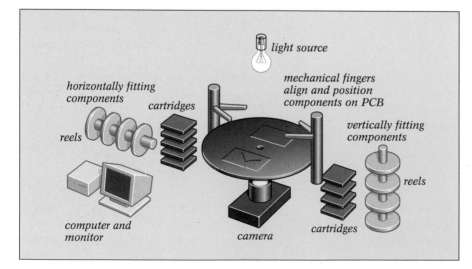

light source

horizontally fitting
components

cartridges

reels

mechanical fingers
align and position
components on PCB

vertically fitting
components

reels

cartridges

computer and
monitor

camera

The hand assembly area.

Diagram showing how the flux-soldering machine works.

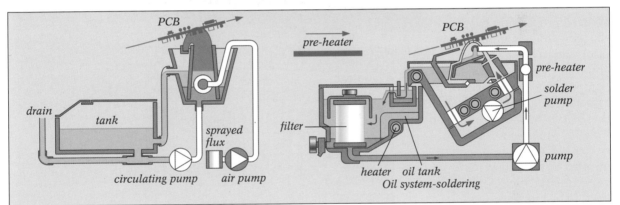

PCB

pre-heater

PCB

pre-heater

solder pump

drain

tank

sprayed flux

filter

circulating pump   air pump

heater   oil tank
Oil system-soldering

pump

You try it ...

Disassemble PCBs from old electrical equipment and investigate the way in which they appear to have been put together.

Testing of completed boards

Visual inspection of the boards is carried out by the operators at various points in the production. The main testing is carried out using an automated test rig which is coupled to a computer. The boards are placed onto a jig and put onto the machine which has a number of spring-loaded gold-plated spikes sticking up. The spikes make contact with the terminals of the board and complete the test circuit.

A pressure plate is brought down onto the board so that good electrical continuity can be maintained during the test period. The computer checks the board and its component values against the software program. The automatic test machine tells the operator what faults it has found, for example, an open circuit, wrong value component or component fitted the wrong way round. The operator corrects any faults, makes good bad joints and clears any short circuits.

Faulty boards are also visually checked by the operator and many minor faults can be corrected by doing this. The completed boards are kept in stock control until they are required for use in the final assembly.

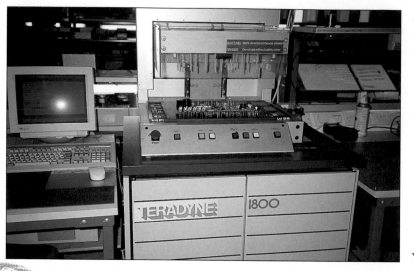

Testing the PCBs.

▼ *Main assembly line.*

Main assembly

When a production batch is started (every Wednesday) information is fed into a computer which works out what components will be needed to make the batch and deducts all these (less the PCB components) from the stock quantity records. In this way the computer can inform the purchasing department which components need to be reordered.

Kits of parts for the week's batch are made available to production. Each person involved in the manufacturing process builds products to a testable stage from a piece-part kit supplied from the stores. This ensures a more interesting work environment than working on the same stage of the process all the time and a greater involvement in the quality of the final product. The kits are made up into the individual items after testing.

Main assembly is a demand-led system because it is based upon a production list of orders which have already been received. There is normally a lead-in time between receipt of orders and assembly and completion of products.

▼ *Wiring PCBs together.*

The cases

The cases used for the products are made from **extruded** aluminium. Aluminium was chosen because it can conduct heat away from the components quickly and, because it is non-magnetic, it does not cause magnetically induced problems from the large transformers used in the systems. The company have to purchase this from Sweden because no British manufacturer could be found to guarantee the specifications required. The extrusions need to be reasonably accurate to accept the fixing of the boards and to look good when set with other units. Any slight warping will be visible to customers when set against other straight lines.

> **You try it ...**
>
> Make a die through which ductile material can be extruded.

> **More about ...** determining fabrication criteria for your own project work page 123.

The aluminium extrusions arrive at the factory, where they are made into cases for Naim Audio Limited, in 5 metre lengths. These are then cut to the required size for particular units. The cases are sent to another company to be anodised and painted. The cases are powder coated with paint and the coating is electrically charged so that it is attracted to the aluminium. The cases are baked and this gives them a very even surface with, in this instance, a crackled effect. This gives a good finish which will not flake off. Paint does not readily adhere to aluminium and anodising is required to allow the bonding to take place. All of the units supplied by the company are finished in black and no other colour is offered. This reduces costs and gives a **corporate** image to the products.

> **You try it ...**
>
> Investigate the ways in which the surfaces of various metals oxidise.
> Find out how aluminium is anodised.
>
> Research the reasons why materials are given different types of finishes and produce a chart showing the results.

> **More about ...** materials page 111; extrusion page 120.

The cases and PCBs are combined and a soak test is carried out. This test involves a four-day period where the units are repeatedly switched on, left for 25 minutes and then switched off for 5 minutes. The test has been devised to show up any faults during the initial operating period when weak or faulty components will fail.

One of the final stages in the production is the addition of the acrylic fronts which are fitted into the extrusions. The acrylic is cut to size and pre-drilled to accept the spindles of the control knobs. The acrylic has five coats of paint applied to it by a silk screen process. No paint is applied where the company **logo** and control information appears. The final coating is a scratch-resistant clear lacquer, similar to that used for plastic spectacle lenses. The front panel is lit from behind which allows the company

▼ *A Naim Audio Limited CD player.*

logo and control information to appear discreetly on the front and gives an effect of depth to the front cover. To prevent damage by scratching, the panel is carefully protected by polythene before it is added.

The control knobs are fitted to the front. The knobs are designed in house and manufactured specifically for the company and are a continuation of the corporate image of the company. All of the units manufactured by Naim Audio Limited have volume controls and on/off switches. However, there are no adjustment controls, for example bass/treble knobs. This keeps the signal clear and unadulterated.

You try it ...

1 Research the properties of acrylic, polythene and a plastic of your choice. Make notes on your findings.
2 Discuss why it might be important to create an overall image of company products.

More about ... plastics page 114.

Summary

In this case study you have looked at:
- **the history and growth of a company;**
- **using scientific principles to design and develop a product;**
- **the importance of a stock control system in demand-led manufacturing and quality control;**
- **using a mixture of computer-controlled and hand assembly in manufacturing;**
- **how different products may be finished to give a common appearance (corporate image).**

You will now be able to complete the tasks below which may form part or all of your coursework.

1 Design and make speaker cabinets.
2 Make a simple PCB. Examine the stages in production. Do a production run for a single item to identify the problems and processes involved for this to be mass produced.

More about ... fabrication page 123.

More about ... determining fabrication criteria for your own project work page 123.

▲ *Naim's products are carefully matched in appearance to fit in with the company's image.*

Product development

This section looks at processes and ideas that are common to many industrial product development projects. You may like to apply some of these ideas in your own design-and-make projects.

Topics covered include:

● developing a specification for project work;
● ergonomics;
● market research;
● quality;
● using computers in design and manufacturing;
● using models.

Developing a specification for project work

This list will help you to produce a **specification** for a product that you are designing and making. The design brief checklist, developed from industrial practice, will also be useful (see page 94).

1 **Identify sources of information.**
These can be the relevant British Standards, makers of specialist fixings and fastenings, technical and specialist literature (such as ergonomic data) or general reference books. You may also need to do some market research.

2 **Establish the working characteristics you require the product to have.**
Think about the service conditions under which your product has to operate.

3 **Prioritise your design criteria.**
Put the things that are most important or essential first.

4 **Develop an initial specification.**
This will take account of product function, safety, quality, reliability, cost factors and the production facilities available to you. Your final fabrication specification will be a developed version of the one you produce at this stage.

5 **Generate a range of ideas for fabricating the product.**
Try not to rule too much out at this stage. Eliminate any obvious 'non-starters' but remember that you might need to investigate new techniques or learn new manufacturing skills.

6 **Evaluate the ideas against your criteria.**
Judge the effectiveness of an idea against the initial specification and your chosen priorities (steps 3 and 4).

7 **Modify the proposal as necessary.**
This may involve 'looping' through steps 1 to 6 again. Time spent here is not wasted as it will improve the final 'build' quality and the reliability of your product.

8 **Produce a model or working prototype.**
This is a particularly important step if you will eventually be manufacturing a large number of products. Engineering designers quite often make **prototypes** to demonstrate their ideas to the company they are designing for.

9 **Draw up the final specification.**
This is an essential part of a **quality assurance** process. It provide the detail that can be used during the process of **quality control**.

Ergonomics

Ergonomic considerations are key factors in product design. Ergonomics applies scientific information about humans to product development.

Anthropometric data

Information about the measurements and physical characteristics of different age groups by gender is collected; this information is called **anthropometric data**.

Designers of products, systems and environments (such as kitchens and playgrounds) have to take account of the physical characteristics of the intended users. Collecting, using, analysing and interpreting anthropometric data helps to develop ergonomic criteria so that the equipment 'fits' the intended users.

In some cases designers may need to make only one or two critical measurements, in others they need to carry out detailed and complex analysis of the data.

The table below is an example of some anthropometric data. This shows the variations in height for different ranges of people. You will notice that there are three figures for each group, labelled 5%le, 50%le, 95%le. These are known as *percentiles*.

Look at the data for the standing height of women aged 19–65 years. The graph on page 95 shows what the percentiles mean.

- Only 5% of women in this age group are below 1505 mm in height. This is known as the 5th percentile, or 5%le for short.
- Only 5% of women in this age group are above 1710 mm. 95% are below this height. This is known as the 95th percentile, or 95%le.
- The majority of women in this age group are close to the average height of 1610 mm. This average is represented by the 50th percentile, or 50%le.

▼ *Extract from an anthropometric data table. All measurements are in mm and are made on people who are not wearing shoes.*

Dimension Measurements in mm	Girls (14–16 years)			Boys (14–16 years)			Women (19–65 years)			Men (19–65 years)		
	5%le	50%le	95%le	5%le	50%le	95%le	5%le	50%le	95%le	5%le	50%le	95%le
A Standing height	1465	1585	1700	1500	1645	1790	1505	1610	1710	1625	1740	1855
B Eye level	1350	1470	1590	1380	1530	1675	1390	1490	1595	1510	1625	1745
C Shoulder height	1180	1285	1395	1215	1345	1480	1210	1310	1410	1310	1415	1525

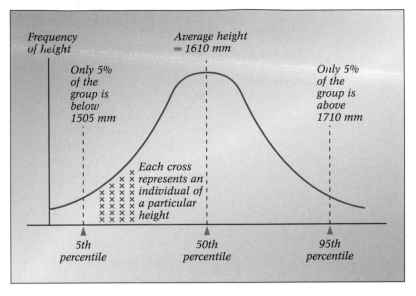

Frequency of height

Average height = 1610 mm

Only 5% of the group is below 1505 mm

Only 5% of the group is above 1710 mm

Each cross represents an individual of a particular height

| 5th percentile | 50th percentile | 95th percentile |

▲ *Explaining percentiles.*

The method of limits

The method of limits is a systematic approach to using anthropometric data to determine the range of people that will be able to use the product (the *limiting users*). It involves defining the boundary conditions that will make an object too small, too large or just the right fit for the majority of people (those who fit between the 5th and 95th percentiles). Designers have to consider the relationship between the dimensions of the user and the dimensions of the product. The three main anthropometric criteria are:

- posture – relating to working conditions, tasks and activities;
- clearance – types of clearance such as leg room, head room;
- reach – the area that a user can reach with the minimum of effort.

The limiting users for posture, clearance and reach ▶ *set the design limits. For posture, the 5%le and 95%le are the limiting users; 90% of users are accommodated between these two measurements. For clearance, the 95%le is the limiting user; the 95% of users smaller than this need not take avoiding action. For reach the limiting user is the 5%le; the 95% of users who can reach further are easily able to reach the back of the table.*

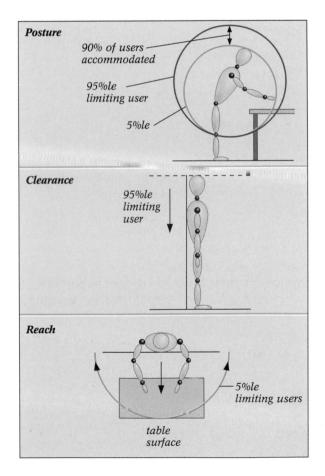

Posture

90% of users accommodated

95%le limiting user

5%le

Clearance

95%le limiting user

Reach

5%le limiting users

table surface

The anthropometric design process

You may find this checklist helpful when thinking about your own projects.

1. Who are you designing the product for (age, gender etc.)?
2. What anthropometric criteria do you have to consider? For example, in the case of a work surface you may decide to consider posture and reach. Working height affects posture and the width of the work surface affects reach. A work surface that is too low can cause stooping and lead to strains in back muscles. A work surface that is too wide could involve stretching to reach the back of it, causing unnecessary strains to the top half of the body.
3. Define the tasks and activities the user will be doing. What are the size and direction of the forces which apply when performing the task or activity? Does the task require precise control?
4. Propose provisional product measurements.
5. Refer to anthropometric data to find out what percentage of the intended users could use the product with the proposed measurements. It is common practice when compiling data tables to take measurements of people who are not wearing shoes and who are wearing minimum clothing. Most people using products will be wearing shoes of some sort, and women may wear higher heels than men. When you are designing you may need to make corrections for this. If the product is for use by people sitting down it may not be such a problem as a product that involves the user standing up.
6. Would enough of the intended users be able to use the product?
7. Modify the measurements as necessary and state the proposed dimensions in terms of the limiting users. For example:

a measurement of … millimetres for the … will accommodate all users between the 5th percentile and 95th percentile.

You try it …

The information below identifies key measurements that allow a user to complete a range of tasks and activities while standing. A production company employs male and female workers aged 19 to 65 to assemble a range of small and large components to make larger consumer electric goods. The assembled goods are light enough to lift off onto a storage pallet. Air-driven (pneumatic) assembly tools connect to control panels at the back of the work surface. Determine the optimum sizes for an assembly bench. Produce a dimensioned line diagram showing all the key dimensions.

▼ *Zone of convenient reach, relating working heights to type of task.*

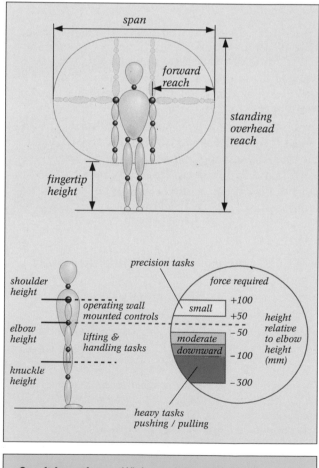

See it in action … Wicksteed page 20; Racal Transcom page 59; President page 69.

Market research

There is no point in going through the product development process if the final result is a product no-one wants! This is where **market research** can help.

Techniques you could use to research your product and its market fall into the four categories on the right.

See it in action ... Arcam page 36.

Primary research
This is information that you gather directly from the public by means of surveys or questionnaires.

Quantitative research
This research technique involves the use of a large representative sample of people. The people selected may be interviewed or asked to fill in detailed and sometimes lengthy forms. The size of the sample affects the statistical reliability of the data collected.

Secondary research
This is information that can be extracted from existing published documents, market surveys, reports and specialist computer databases.

Qualitative research
This is a more-focused 'in depth' technique. Small groups of people or individuals are consulted in order to find out about their attitudes and responses to particular products. The information is more difficult to collect and interpret. It is subjective because you will be canvassing opinions and attitudes rather than verifiable facts (objective research).

Survey and questionnaire design

With the exception of secondary research, you will need to design either a survey or questionnaire to collect and record information for future analysis.

The information you collect is data. The analysis of the information that you do is known as *data analysis*. You need to plan your questions carefully so that you collect useful and relevant information. There are four different types of question that you might consider.

Closed questions provide 'yes/no' type responses, or offer a limited choice of answer.

Open-ended questions are useful for finding out about attitudes and opinions, but they produce a wide variety of responses that take time to interpret and sort out.

Structured questions break a long and complicated question into manageable parts.

Rating questions use a scaling system and give a quick indication of attitudes and opinions. Answers can be coded and analysed numerically, for example, '68% of people think that ...'

You try it ...

Look at the following questionnaire about a new CD player; imagine that the questionnaire is being used at an electrical superstore after a salesperson has demonstrated the player. Which kinds of questions does the questionnaire use? Can you think of ways of improving the questionnaire to make it easier to understand and use?

1 Had you heard about the new CD player before today? yes/no

*2 Do you like the sound of the player?
a little / a lot / neither like nor dislike / not at all.*

3 What do you think about the rear panel connections?

4 What do you like about the control panel?

*5 Describe the look of the product. Is it:
interesting/dull
technical/non-technical to look at
pleasing to the eye/not pleasing to the eye?*

6 Which face sums up how you feel overall about the player?

▲ *The five standard 'smiley' faces.*

Cost–benefit analysis

This can be used to look at customer requirements for a product in terms of price and non-price factors. Non-price factors can be technical quality or service. Cost–benefit analysis enables you to compare the relative importance of these factors.

Price factors include:

- indirect costs of purchasing,
- life cycle costs reflecting the whole life cost of the product, allowing for running costs, servicing, breakdown and replacement part costs, depreciation and disposal costs.

Non-price technical factors include:

- performance in operation,
- reliability,
- durability,
- ease of use and maintenance,
- safety considerations,
- appearance,
- materials and finishes,
- flexible usage,
- packaging and presentation at point of sale.

Non-price service factors include:

- the quality of after-sale servicing,
- the accuracy of delivery dates, and
- dealer training programmes.

Quality

Until quite recently calling something a 'quality product' simply meant the product was expensive. However, manufacturers are increasingly finding a different view of quality useful in judging both products and services. In this view, quality products or services:

- meet a clear defined need, use or purpose;
- satisfy the expectations of existing or potential customers in performance characteristics, visual characteristics (style, colour, etc.);
- comply with requirements of society in terms of statutory regulations, laws, rules, health and safety regulations, environmental considerations;
- conserve energy and materials;
- are available at competitive prices that will make the company a profit.

Manufacturers and customers might have different opinions about what makes a quality product. A perfect product does not have guaranteed sales. Consumers can easily reject a perfectly manufactured product because it does not meet their requirements. Manufacturers need to find out their customers' definition of quality.

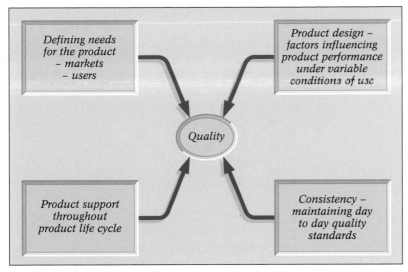

▲ *Factors in product quality.*

Quality assurance occurs throughout the production process, from goods and raw materials coming into the factory to the customer receiving the product. It is described in the British Standard document BS 4778 as

all those planned and systematic actions necessary to provide adequate confidence that a product or service will satisfy given requirements for quality ... Unless given requirements fully reflect the needs of the user, quality assurance will not be complete.

Quality assurance and quality control

All work is achieved as the result of a process. In any process there are points at which quality assessments and measurements can be made. For example, measurements could be made on any of the following:

- inputs to the process – e.g. data, components, mechanisms, finance;
- the process itself – a 'value-adding' stage that involves people, equipment and other resources;
- outputs from the process – e.g. invoices, products, devices, services.

Quality is achieved when the results of these measurements are interpreted and used to shape future work practice.

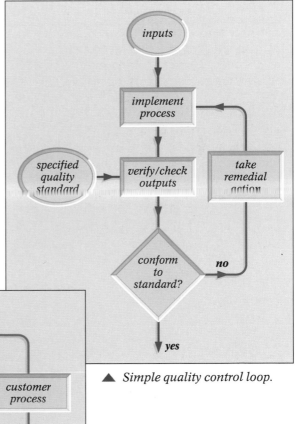

▲ *Simple quality control loop.*

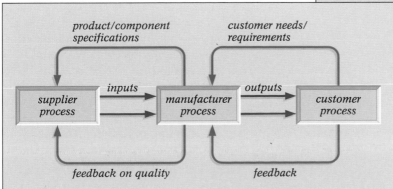

◄ *Specifications and feedback on quality are important throughout a manufacturing chain.*

Quality control takes place at the end of each part of the manufacturing process. It is the procedures, techniques and activities that a company will put in place for inspecting products and detecting those that are not up to standard.

Quality systems

The organisational structures, procedures, processes and resources needed to build quality into a product or service make up a *quality system*. A quality system has several key quality objectives including fitness for purpose, performance, safety and reliability. BS 5750: 1987 outlines the elements of a quality loop. (NB You may come across references to ISO 9000. In some, but not all, cases this is identical to BS 5750. It will eventually replace the British Standard.)

BS 5750 specifies a number of actions or procedures that a company has to take in order to achieve a consistent and acceptable standard of quality. All companies are audited and monitored every six months to check that they are maintaining the required levels of quality. The company must have a *quality manual*. The manual specifies:

- quality objectives for the product, its parts and manufacture;
- clearly identified job responsibilities within an organisational structure;
- procedures, equipment and instructions for methods of working;
- the stages when, and how, testing, inspection and quality audits need to be made;
- ways of dealing with any identified problem or modification;
- other measures necessary to meet the quality objectives;
- how quality records and charts should be kept.

▼ *Quality loop.*

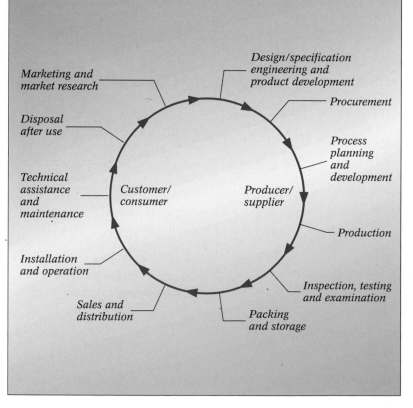

Marketing and market research

Disposal after use

Technical assistance and maintenance

Installation and operation

Sales and distribution

Customer/consumer

Design/specification engineering and product development

Procurement

Process planning and development

Producer/supplier

Production

Inspection, testing and examination

Packing and storage

See it in action ... Wicksteed page 15.

Quality audits

Quality audits are planned to determine how effectively the quality management system and its sub-systems are maintaining the quality objectives. They are carried out by trained people who are not directly involved in the activity or area being audited. All reports are written up and have to be available to independent reviewers for evaluation.

Quality in design

Quality in design provides a regular evaluation at significant control points, which are

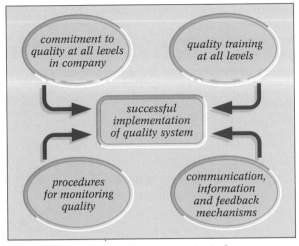

▲ *Implementing quality systems in industry.*

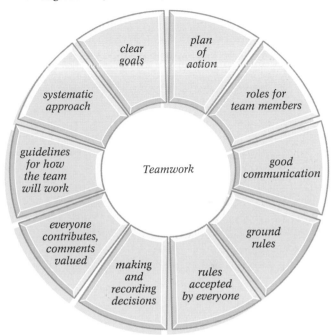

▼ *Ingredients for successful teamwork.*

sometimes called **milestones**. When each design development milestone is reached a design review is written up. (This is not the same as a project progress review which concerns itself with costs and time deadlines.) A design review will include representatives from all the sections involved in a project.

See it in action ... Arcam page 43.

Quality in marketing

Quality also applies in the **marketing** of a product. In many companies the marketing department take the lead in determining quality requirements. Their market knowledge helps to determine in which sectors there is a demand for a product. They can also clearly and accurately express their customers' specific requirements. This can be done through the product brief which translates the needs into a set of technical specifications which the designers begin to work with.

See it in action ... Arcam page 40.

Using teamwork to achieve quality

To achieve quality requires teamwork. The whole workforce has to fully and actively co-operate through manufacturing philosophies such as *total quality management* (TQM) and continuous improvement (CI). *Quality circles* or *quality action teams* (QUATs), which are teams of people brought together to solve design or production problems in order to improve levels of quality, are an essential part of quality systems.

QUATs can be a group from the same area in a factory or have a range of different skills. One person working on their own may produce a good idea; working in a group means that ideas can develop more fully, often in a shorter time. This is the idea behind **concurrent engineering**.

You may find that you can improve the quality of your own and other students' projects by forming simple quality teams of three or four people. You can each take it in turns to describe your progress and any problems you are having. Sometimes four minds working on a problem can be more effective than working on your own. Remember the need to record all the decisions and why they were taken.

See it in action ... Wicksteed page 15; Arcam page 40.

You try it ...

You work for a company that makes promotional gifts. You have won an order for a batch of 3000 products. You are the leader of the team taking responsibility for the quality of the product, which is made up of a series of components. One of the components is shown.

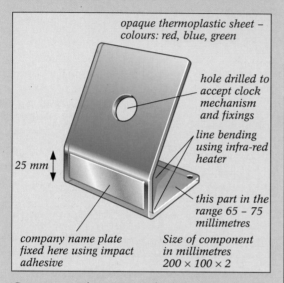

opaque thermoplastic sheet – colours: red, blue, green

hole drilled to accept clock mechanism and fixings

line bending using infra-red heater

25 mm

this part in the range 65 – 75 millimetres

company name plate fixed here using impact adhesive

Size of component in millimetres 200 × 100 × 2

Component of promotional gift.

Look at the design of the component and:
- identify and list the **critical quality assurance points** and at what point in the manufacturing process they will occur,
- for each critical point outline the methods, systems or procedures that need to be in place in order to determine if the product is fit to pass onto the next stage of manufacture,
- prepare and write up your quality assurance plan.

In working on this project you might like to try a technique known as '1–2–4–snowball' to help you to sort out your own ideas or to make sure that everyone's ideas are considered by your group.

One-two-four-snowball. ▶

Balancing costs, benefits and quality

There are certain risks, costs and benefits involved in quality that a company has to consider both for themselves and their customers.

Risks

Risks incurred by not employing quality assurance systems could include:

- loss of image, reputation or market share;
- complaints and legal claims;
- inefficient use of human and financial resources.

For a customer the product or service may be harmful to health or unsafe or generally lack the performance they require.

Costs

Costs are incurred by:

- marketing and product development problems;
- unsatisfactory materials or components that cause re-working, repair, warranty claims, replacement or re-processing;
- loss of production time in 'making good' defective products.

The customer may withdraw from contracts or fail to buy the company's products in the future. Breakdowns in service can cause adverse publicity and lead to a negative brand image.

Internal quality costs are those arising from reaching and maintaining specified quality outcomes. Preventative measures to avoid failures in the first place add extra costs. Appraisal costs arise from testing, inspection

One	On your own write down three or four ideas of the ways in which a quality action team can help you. Put these into order, the most important first.
Two	Join with another person to discuss your ideas and agree on two ideas each.
Four	Join with another pair to agree on one way to help each person.
Snowball	List the key action points that all your team agreed.

and examination which takes time and often involves specialist testing equipment or computer software.

External quality costs arise when the company has to demonstrate and prove that their product or service is up to standard. Assessment and testing by independent bodies is an essential element for the marketing of manufactured products. A company manufacturing electric consumer goods such as washing machines or toasters is unable to sell its products without acceptable electrical testing. A favourable report from a specialist consumer magazine or a newspaper can significantly boost the sales of individual products.

Benefits

Benefits to a company are increases in profitability and market share, quality brand image and strong customer base.

> **You try it ...**
>
> In most projects you have to balance cost, time and quality. The balance changes according to the project. Which of the following projects would fit each situation shown in the diagram?
> - Safety alarm
> - Walking aid
> - Child's toy
> - Ball-point pen
> - Ready-to-wear clothes
> - Mass produced furniture
> - Individually designed furniture

Using computers in design and manufacturing

Computers play a major role in industrial manufacturing and commerce. Computers are revolutionary because they are the first machines to have a memory that can store instructions and information. A computer program either provides the necessary information or converts data signals sent from input devices such as scanners and video cameras. A program can also change the way in which a computer functions. All computer systems contain certain basic elements, as the diagram on page 104 suggests.

Computer-aided design (CAD)

For many designers the computer keyboard, mouse, graphics tablet and display screen are tools which have replaced pencil, paper and the drawing board.

CAD programs use specialised software to create mathematical models that represent the characteristics and geometry of an object. Co-ordinates give points on

▼ *Product scenarios.*

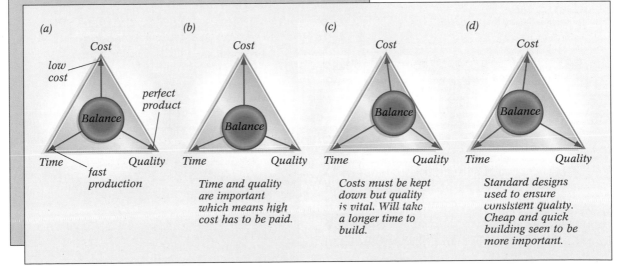

(a)	(b)	(c)	(d)
low cost / *perfect product* / *fast production*	Time and quality are important which means high cost has to be paid.	Costs must be kept down but quality is vital. Will take a longer time to build.	Standard designs used to ensure consistent quality. Cheap and quick building seen to be more important.

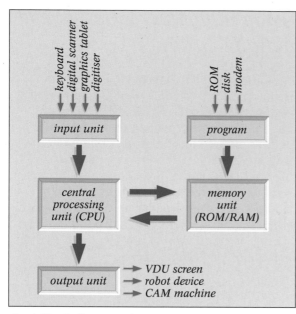

keyboard
digital scanner
graphics tablet
digitiser

ROM
disk
modem

input unit

program

central
processing
unit (CPU)

memory
unit
(ROM/RAM)

output unit

→ VDU screen
→ robot device
→ CAM machine

▲ *A block diagram of a computer system.*

the object a grid position which can be related to other points by mathematical formulae and geometric calculations. Once the co-ordinates of the points are determined, the computer is able to analyse the shape and design of an object. It builds up a mathematical description of the shape which is stored in the computer's memory as a set of codes. When the object is moved or rotated, the computer uses this numerical data to reposition the object on screen.

Designers also use automated drafting programs that rely on interactive computer graphics. All the basic graphic elements such as points, lines, circles and tangents have precise geometric relationships which the computer stores in memory as numerical information. Objects are drawn by combining these basic elements. Elements are easy to move, rotate, mirror or scale larger or smaller. Most programs allow designers to zoom in on specific details of the design allowing very detailed work. This form of computer drawing technique is often referred to as an object-oriented graphics system.

You try it …

Investigate the operational capabilities of a CAD system or computer drawing system by preparing a two- or three-dimensional computer graphic representation of an object or product you have made or intend to make.

See it in action … Margaret Turner page 7; Racal Transcom page 60.

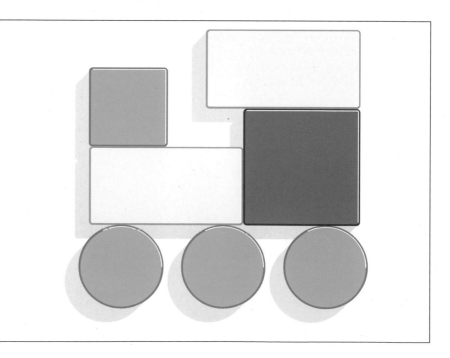

How a complicated ▶ *shape can be built up using simple geometric shapes.*

CAD/CAM systems

The link between CAD and CAM (computer-aided manufacturing) is providing one of the major driving forces of a new industrial revolution. Mechanical engineering and electronic design have been the major users of CAD/CAM. Other industries like the furniture industry are catching up quickly and in some cases pioneering new techniques and applications (for example, CAD is used in car design).

Desktop manufacturing is a technique that integrates design and manufacturing. The computer can be used as a design tool which produces concept or manufacturing drawings. A change of instruction can send the machining data to an automatic production machine.

▲ *Using CAD in car design.*

▼ *CAD/CAM machine in use in a school workshop.*

The production advantages of CAD/CAM
CAD/CAM systems provide:

- rapid retrieval of information from a variety of sources around the world including **databases**, spreadsheets and specialist computer libraries,
- quick calculations and the power to analyse data;
- the flexibility to change or modify designs on screen which avoids the cost of producing prototype models;
- faster and more accurate drawings using plotters and printers;
- drawings which can be stored, retrieved and modified electronically;
- digital information which is easily shared using devices like networks and modems;
- data which can be transferred electronically – a designer may be in one country, the manufacturing company in another;
- improved design 'turn-round time' which reduces product development costs;
- a consistent, reliable and repeatable quality of product;
- increased operational flexibility and elimination of operator error;
- reduced labour costs, although the initial cost of industrial machines can be very high.

You try it ...

Make three lists of products in wood, metal and plastics that you think might make good use of CAD techniques. Choose one product from each list. Prepare a short report with illustrations explaining the advantages that CAD/CAM would provide for making that product over traditional design and make techniques.

Dimensional co-ordination – using CAD/CAM in practice

Dimensional co-ordination is a design system which uses standard anthropometric data. Kitchen design companies, for example, almost always adopt this 'modular' approach.

The whole range of kitchen units is designed to a standard size and proportional to each other – hence the term 'dimensional co-ordination'. A single-door cabinet may be offered in several design options – it may have drawers, one shelf instead of drawers or be one large storage space. A double-door cabinet may have drawers one side and shelves the other. These standard-size units match in with the standard sizes of white goods such as washing machines, refrigerators and cookers. This is an ideal situation for using CAD systems.

▼ *Examples of dimensional co-ordination.*

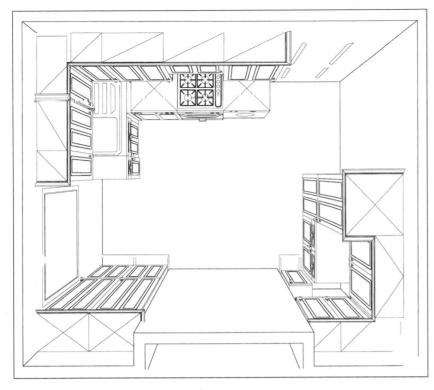

◀ *A computer print-out of a kitchen installation.*

Large companies such as MFI can produce plans, elevations, three-dimensional representations and much more.

Once the customer decides on a layout the computer database automatically prints out the required parts, stock lists and the total cost of the package. If the customer decides to buy the package, details can be transferred electronically to the storage warehouse for the customer to collect. If the units are not in stock an order is raised which can be sent directly to the manufacturing company. The same data is also used to prepare the customer's sales invoice and product guarantee forms. This is an example of an integrated design system.

> **You try it ...**
> Design a set of nets to be used as a CAD computer library to illustrate a range of kitchen/office furniture.

The design and finish of the doors on one kitchen range may be different to those on another range, but the cupboard carcasses they attach to are all made to the same sizes. The hinges that hold the doors on are of a standard size and fitted in similar positions which make it an ideal opportunity to use CAM. All the sizes can be stored in a database, or the dimensioned unit shapes for cupboards, drawer units and so on can be held in a computer graphics library on hard disk or a dedicated CD-ROM.

The designer inputs the sizes of the space the units are going into and then designs the kitchen arrangement by **downloading** and positioning the standard units on screen as required. The electronic pictures are easy to move around and place. Different combinations can be worked out for the customer to look at.

> **See it in action ...** Wicksteed page 18; President Office Furniture page 79.

> **You try it ...**
> Collect furniture product brochures from two large DIY stores. Compare the sizes of similar units and pieces of furniture as well as the range of design options offered. If you were designing the following pieces of furniture for domestic use, what overall sizes – length, width and depth (in millimetres) – would you specify? Don't forget to include the dimensions of the materials you might be using.
> - Bedside cabinet
> - Wall-mounted double-door kitchen cabinet
> - Floor-mounted four-drawer kitchen unit
> - Kitchen table
> - Open shelf system to store 60 CDs

Using models

A model is increasingly seen as a development tool – part of the process of design rather than just a realistic representation of the end product. In industry, model shops often provide this kind of specialist help. For example, they can produce quick sketch models in a type of polystyrene foam from the initial drawings, enabling the designer to see how the design would work in three dimensions.

Another type of model focuses on ergonomic and mechanical factors – these 'test rigs' are assemblies that perform as required, but may not have any visual or aesthetic quality. From these models the designer can find out whether the design will be suitable for people or whether the mechanical design is appropriate.

Once a design has been chosen, a presentation 'block model' may be produced. This model aims to show as closely as possible the external form, details, colour, texture, etc. of the proposed final product. Models to show any relevant engineering details will also be produced at this stage.

A small number of precise component parts may then be manufactured as resin castings from patterns and silicone rubber moulds by the model shop. These can be used to carry out fit, form and function tests.

The photos that follow show examples of different types of models.

See it in action ... President Office Furniture page 73.

◀ Visual model of Sanitana European sink-top.

▼ Model of a retail system for ICI Dulux.

▲ New concept model of a personal stereo.

Prototype of a Samsonite attaché case and accessories.

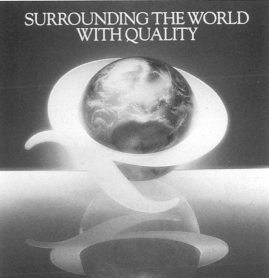

Advertising model for East McFarland.

SURROUNDING THE WORLD WITH QUALITY

ISO 9002
FIRST REGISTRATION
IN CHLORIDE

IN SULPHATE

In 1989, Tioxide became the first titanium dioxide manufacturer in the world to achieve registration to ISO 9002 for both chloride and sulphate processes.
Today, Tioxide is actively pursuing world-wide registration.

The control, discipline and experience that have been gained by registration are now being applied to our environmental and safety programmes and to the many other activities that are an integral part of our vision of Total Quality Management.

Tioxide Group PLC Tioxide House 137-143 Hammersmith Road London W14 0QL

Tioxide

Quality in Partnership

CERTIFICATE NUMBERS
Q6641/FM39359
FM39652/FM39047
FM1992/M10177

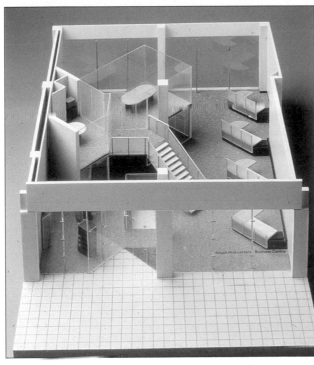

Architectural scale model for the Post Office.

◀ *Block models of Philips jug kettle.*

▼ *Engineering prototype of computer monitor.*

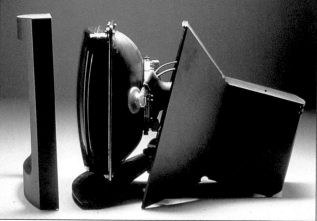

◀ *Packaging models of Caliner toiletries range.*

◀ *Exhibition model of guitar synthesizer for Design Council.*

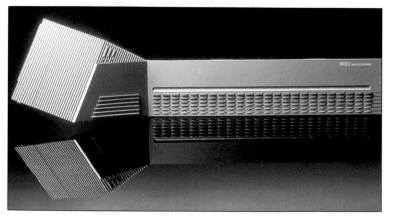

Materials

Designing or improving a product requires a knowledge of materials and their properties in order to select, process and finish them to meet design criteria. There are over 80 000 materials to choose from.

Classifying and selecting materials

Resistant materials can be divided into four main types:

- metals and alloys;
- composites, manufactured boards and concrete;
- polymers – synthetic plastics;
- ceramics (combinations of metallic and non-metallic elements).

Each type of material has a different internal structure and hence different properties and characteristics. These affect how a material can be processed and finished.

The choice of material for a product will depend on the product's particular requirements. These requirements fall under the four headings opposite.

The final choice of material for a particular product will almost always involve a compromise between the various requirements.

Physical and mechanical properties of materials

You will need to consider the following properties when making your choice of material:

- load bearing properties;
- corrosion resistance;
- creep resistance ('creep' is where the length of the material increases under a tensile force);
- density (mass per volume; this affects a component's weight);
- elasticity;

Service requirements
– physical characteristics
– mechanical properties

Economic requirements
– availability of material
– cost of material
– cost of machining
– cost of joining
– cost of casting or working
– time taken to fabricate

Fabrication requirements
– malleability
– machinability
– ductility
– castability
– ease of joining
– response to heat treatment
– availability of manufacturing resources

Specific component requirements
– appearance
– shape
– function
– performance
– quantity
– environmental impact

- electrical properties (whether the material is a conductor, insulator, or semi-conductor, dependent on its electrical resistance);
- fatigue resistance;
- hardness (a measure of the material's ability to withstand being cut, dented or scratched);
- heat resistance;
- magnetic properties;
- strength (how good the material is at resisting being deformed when acted on by different forces – compressive, tensile, shear, torsional);
- thermal conductivity (a measure of how quickly heat travels through the material);
- thermal expansion (a measure of how much the material expands given a certain amount of heat);
- toughness (a measure of how much energy is required to break the material).

Metals and alloys

Hundreds of millions of tonnes of metals are used every year in a wide range of industrial applications. Metals are a large group of elements that have certain physical and chemical properties and characteristics in common, such as the ability to conduct heat and electricity. They range from the familiar iron, aluminium, copper and lead, through to the precious metals gold, silver and platinum.

Classifying metals

Metallic materials fall into two groups: ferrous (containing iron), and non-ferrous.

Ferrous metals include:

- wrought iron;
- cast irons;
- carbon steels, including high carbon steel and mild steel;
- alloy steels, including stainless steel.

Non-ferrous metals include:

- lead, tin, copper, zinc, aluminium;
- metals used in small amounts (chromium, tantalum, mercury, silver, gold, platinum, etc.);
- 'new' metals (vanadium, niobium, zirconium, etc.).

Properties of metals

An important characteristic of most metals is that they can be *worked* – they will generally change shape rather than break when they are placed under pressure or impact from tools and machines. Metals that can be hammered or beaten into sheets are called *malleable*, and those that can be drawn into wire are called *ductile*.

Certain properties, such as hardness, are not shared by all metals. Some, such as lead, are soft enough to be scratched by a fingernail or deformed by hand. One familiar metal, mercury, is liquid at ordinary temperatures. Almost all metals can be oxidised under mild conditions.

The atomic structure of metals is **crystalline** – hexagonal, face centred cubic or body centred cubic.

▼ *Crystal lattice structures.*

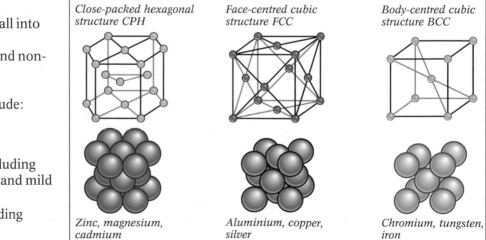

Close-packed hexagonal structure CPH	Face-centred cubic structure FCC	Body-centred cubic structure BCC
Zinc, magnesium, cadmium	Aluminium, copper, silver	Chromium, tungsten, iron

Alloys

An alloy is produced when metals are combined with one or more elements. Alloys have a variety of compositions and generally have physical properties which differ considerably from the base metals. By careful choice of composition, alloys that have great hardness, toughness, mechanical strength and resistance to corrosion can be made.

Common alloys include brass (copper and zinc), bronze (copper and tin), mild steel (iron and carbon), stainless steel (iron, chromium, nickel, and carbon) and soft solders (lead and tin).

Plumber's solder is high in lead and low in tin which gives it important mechanical jointing properties. Electrician's solder uses the same elements but is high in tin and low in lead (see page 51). This combination improves the fluidity and increases the speed of solidification to prevent the heat damaging sensitive electronic components.

Wood

Wood is a hard, fibrous substance. Wood cells consist of two chemicals: *cellulose* and *lignin* which is an organic resin. Wood is a natural polymer.

Wood is classified as *hardwood* or *softwood*. Hardwoods generally come from either deciduous or evergreen broad-leafed trees, such as beech and oak. Softwoods are generally obtained from conifers such as cedar, fir and pine. The terms softwood or hardwood describe how the tree grows, rather than the type of timber produced from it. Balsa is a hardwood that is light in weight and soft to work. Pitch pine, a softwood, is heavy and very difficult to work.

The properties of wood explain its role as a major manufacturing material. It is easy to fasten, shape and reshape, smooth, and it is long lasting (wooden structures which are many hundreds of years old have remained in good condition with minimal care). Wood is a poor conductor of heat and is therefore useful as an insulator. It does not conduct electricity. Wood can be recycled many times.

The properties of wood differ from species to species which leads to a range of different uses. The hardness of wood refers to the resistance of wood to a saw across the grain. Hardness is primarily dependent on weight, degree of seasoning and the structure of the wood.

Structurally, wood is further classified into *sapwood* and *heartwood*. Sapwood is the part of the wood that conducts water. Heartwood provides structural support for the tree and usually makes better timber than sapwood. It is often drier, has a richer colour than sapwood and is more resistant to decay.

Conversion is the term which is used to describe the sawing of logs into timber. Plain sawing is the simplest, quickest and cheapest method of converting logs into boards. Quarter or radial sawing means that fewer and narrower boards are obtainable which means that radially cut timber is more expensive. The method of sawing determines what the grain patterns of the wood will look like, what it can be used for and how it will react in different environmental conditions. Wood grain, the arrangement of wood cells, is specific to each species of tree and is often seen as a desirable decorative property. Quarter sawing generally produces the best grain patterns.

Composites

Veneers, chipboard, and plywood are used in construction, for making and facing large surface areas, and in the manufacture of furniture. Veneer and plywood are both thin pieces of wood which are glued together to form stronger products. Chipboard (particleboard) uses wood chips and shavings with a bonding agent to form panels. Veneer is a thin slice of a log cut in sheet form. Once cut, the more decorative veneers, especially from choice hardwoods such as cherry, walnut, and rosewood, are used in furniture manufacture or other uses where appearance is important. Plywood is a strong, durable manufactured board made by gluing veneers together in alternate layers with the grain of one layer at ninety degrees to that of the next. The adhesive used determines whether the plywood can be used inside or outside.

Plastics

Plastics are a very large group of synthetic (manufactured) materials with structures based on carbon. Plastics are also called polymers because they are made of extremely long chains of carbon atoms. An important characteristic of plastics is that they can be readily moulded into finished products by the application of heat. Thousands of plastics have been manufactured since the 1940s and these have been used in a wide range of products, including machine gears, artificial hearts and bonding cements for such things as aircraft structures.

Resistant plastic materials are divided into two main categories: **thermoset** and **thermoplastic**. Other categories of plastic are *elastomers*, *foams* and **composites**.

Thermoset and thermoplastic materials

When a thermoset is heated it softens and can be moulded into a shape. It undergoes a chemical change which is irreversible. Further heating will not soften the material and at high temperatures it will become brittle and start to degrade. Under tensile forces they behave like brittle metals or ceramics. They have low ductility and poor impact properties.

A thermoplastic material will soften when heated and harden when cooled. This process is repeatable and can be likened to the melting of wax.

It is not necessary for all the monomer units in a polymer to be identical. Two kinds of

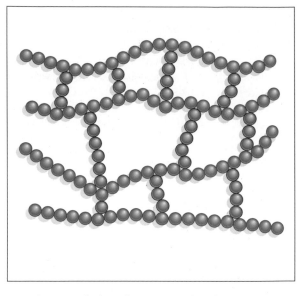

▲ *The cross-linking between molecules in thermosets forms a rigid network structure.*

monomers may be blended into a polymer chain, as in the case of styrene and butadiene. Such plastics are called *copolymers*. **ABS plastic** is a copolymer of the monomers acrylonitrile, butadiene and styrene. Copolymerisation of two or more monomers is similar in effect to the alloying of two or more metals. Pure polystyrene is brittle, but if a percentage of butadiene monomers is incorporated into the chain of styrene monomers, a high-impact grade of polystyrene results.

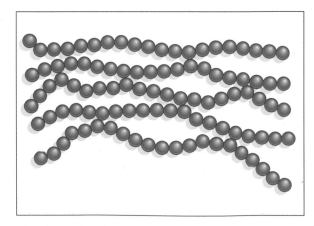

▲ *The molecules in a thermoplastic are in linear chains.*

Name	Thermal properties	General properties	Uses
Polymethyl methacrylate PMMA (Acrylic) Available as: • cast acrylic • extruded acrylic	Thermoplastic Rigid up to 85°C Elastic mouldable range 120–185°C	Hard and stiff, with good flexibility Excellent optical properties; resists weathering by sunlight. Easy to fabricate by solvent cements. Machines and polishes well. Available in a range of opaque and translucent colours and transparent sheets.	Windows, fabricated signs, point of sale displays, baths, furniture cabinets and containers, vehicle lights, extruded shapes and sections.
Cellulose Acetate Available in powder, sheet and rod (extruded sections for tool handles)	Thermoplastic	Tough, hard and light in weight. Easy to machine. Can be made flexible.	Telephone housings, tool handles, pen bodies, knobs and lids, photographic film.
Polyethylene (PE) (Polyethene) Available in five grades – most common are: • low density (LDPE) • high density (HDPE)	Thermoplastic Softening temperature 60°C rising according to density of the plastic	Soft, flexible, waxy material. Good chemical resistance but attracts dust. Has to be stabilised to avoid degradation by sunlight. The higher the density the harder and stiffer the plastic becomes.	Squeezable bottles and children's toys. Plastic sacks and covering sheets. Film for packaging. Milk crates, bottles and barrels.
Polystyrene (PS) Available in powder, granules and sheet forms. Can be modified to produce a foam.	Thermoplastic Rigid up to 85°C. Very small elastic range limits. Thermoforming possibilities extrusion and vacuum forming.	A low cost plastic. Thermoforming range is very small. Poor resistance to sunlight and solvents. A clear, hard, brittle material that has excellent optical properties. Available in a range of colours. Can be toughened to increase impact strength.	Low cost, disposable items such as food and drink containers. Toughened polystyrene can be used for toys and the lining inside refrigerators. Foams used for insulation and packaging
Polyvinyl chloride (PVC) Available in rigid and plasticised (flexible) forms.	Thermoplastic. Rigid up to 85°C Elastic range 100–145°C	Flexible forms: soft, good electrical insulators, high chemical resistance. Rigid forms: stiff, hard, tough but light in weight, high resistance to to chemical attack. All PVCs are available in a wide range of colours. Difficult to join by solvents, has to be hot air welded.	Flexible form: shower curtains, hoses and electrical insulation. Rigid form: pipes, guttering bottles, roofing sheets, window frames, curtain rails.
Polyamide (nylon) Available in rod, tube and sheet	Thermoplastic Softens between 185–220°C	Nylon is classed as one of the engineering plastics. It is hard, tough, rigid and self-lubricating. Crystalline structure that is wear and friction resistant. High melting point. Easy to machine and resistant to chemicals.	Machine parts such as gears, cams, bearings. Clothing and general domestic items. Casings for power tools, car parts and electrical components

Name	Thermal properties	General properties	Uses
Acrylonitrile butadiene styrene (ABS)	Thermoplastic Rigid up to 100°C Elastic range 105–130°C	Hard wearing engineering plastic with high impact strength. Can be joined by solvents or hot air welding. Scratch resistant with high surface finish. Resistant to chemical attack. Available in limited colour range.	Heavy duty piping for drains, waste and vent pipes. Parts for cars. Enclosures for electrical appliances. Camera cases, toys and safety helmets.
Polycarbonate (PC) Available mainly in sheet form.	Thermoplastic Rigid up to 175°C Limited elastic range	High resistance to impact and effects of fire. Transparent and stable plastic. Can be screen printed and is weather resistant. Easy to join using solvent cements and mechanical fixings.	Vandal-proof glazing, safety hats, visors, and machine guards. Signs and displays.
Polypropylene (PP) Available in powder, granules, sheets, rods.	Thermoplastic Rigid up to 140°C Very small elastic range	A light engineering plastic used in specialist applications. It is a hard, strong crystalline plastic. Can be brittle at low temperatures. Resistant to chemical attack. Can be joined by hot air welding. It is pliable and resistant to shock loading. Good resistance to repeated loading.	Mechanical fixings such as rivets, nuts, bolts, screws and hinges. Crates, pipes and car parts. Packaging film and medical equipment such as syringes. Flexible ropes, string and nets.
Polyester resin (PR) Available in liquids and pastes.	Thermoset Hardened by the addition of a catalyst (curing).	Good electrical insulator with heat and chemical resistance. Excellent weathering properties. Easy to colour using pigments and dyes. Brittle unless reinforced by fibres. Contracts on curing.	Castings. Composite materials reinforced by glass for carbon fibres, for boat bodies, furniture and containers.
Epoxy resin (ER) Epoxide	Thermoset Resin and hardener mixed together Hardens over time	Good chemical and wear resistance. Reinforcing with glass fibres increases strength. Heat resistance to 250°C. Excellent adhesive properties,	Surface coating, castings, adhesives.
Formaldehydes Urea-formaldehyde (UF) Melamine-formaldehyde (MF) Phenol-formaldehyde (PF)	Thermoset	UF is stiff, hard and brittle, heat resistant. MF is stiff, hard, strong, stain and chemical resistant. PF is stiff, hard, brittle (strength improved by laminating with paper and fabric).	UF – electrical fittings, adhesives. MF – tableware (knives, forks), decorative laminates, paints. PF – electrical fittings, parts of electrical appliances, bottle tops and laminates.

Elastomers

Elastomers are elastic substances that can recover their original dimensions after being stretched. The large group of elastomer materials includes natural rubber as well as a growing number of synthetic rubbers. All elastomers are capable of large extensions before breaking. The most common synthetic elastomer is the general-purpose rubber SBR (styrene-butadiene rubber) used in car and lorry tyres. Other elastomers are used in textiles, socks and footwear and the production of rubber foams such as urethane.

Foams

The first of the foamed plastics to be developed was polystyrene (Styrofoam). It is commonly used as building insulation, flotation devices and prototype modelling. Polystyrene foams are either extruded with a blowing agent or created in a mould by using expandable beads to make the familiar white coffee cup you see in cafes and fast food restaurants. Foams can have open or closed cells. Open cells absorb water, closed cells do not. Polystyrene, polyurethane (for insulation) and ABS foams have three principal uses: thermal insulation, cushioning materials and structural materials.

Composite materials

Most plastic products are manufactured from composite materials, for example fibreglass-reinforced polyester (GRP). Polyvinyl chloride floor tiles have a clay filler to reduce moisture absorption and improve surface gloss. Plastic foams are composites of plastic and gas cells. To obtain strength, which is comparable to that of metals, in a plastic, reinforcing fibres must be used. CFRPs are high strength, low weight, carbon fibre reinforced plastics.

Polymer technology is a constantly developing field of study which makes it difficult to make general statements about plastic materials. These properties apply to most plastics:

1 they have low strength (about one-sixth the strength of structural steel);
2 they have low stiffness (modulus of elasticity) except for reinforced plastics;
3 they have a tendency to 'creep' (length increases under a tensile force);
4 except for formaldehyde plastics, they have low hardness;
5 they are of low density;
6 at low temperatures they become brittle and at moderate temperatures they lose strength and hardness;
7 plastics are flammable, although many plastics do not burst into flames;
8 they have outstanding electrical characteristics such as electrical resistance (insulators);
9 ultra-violet (UV) light causes some plastics to degrade;
10 most plastics are highly resistant to chemical attack.

Materials processing

Materials processing is the name manufacturers use to describe the handling of the range of materials needed to make a product.

In your design work it may be helpful to group the processes for making things under separate headings – wood, metal, plastics and so on. An alternative is to link similar processes.

The main materials processing techniques are (in alphabetical order):

casting and moulding
• sand,
• metal die,
• lost wax,
• plastic resin,
• shell moulding

finishing processes
• wood,
• metal,
• plastic,
• corrosion proofing

forming
• forging,
• bending,
• drawing,
• extrusion,
• pressing,
• rolling

laminating

machining

Casting and moulding

A whole range of materials including plastics, metals and ceramics can be cast into a variety of shapes.

Casting involves a fluid material being poured into a mould of the required shape where it becomes solid. *Injection moulding* is a similar technique. It uses pressure to force the fluid plastic into a metal mould.

See it in action . . . Racal Transcom page 60; President Office Furniture page 77.

Lost wax casting is the most accurate and reliable method of producing fine detail and complex shapes, especially in a production run. It is also known as centrifugal casting, vacuum casting or investment casting. It dates back more than 5000 years. It is used almost exclusively by the jewellery and dental trades which use precious metals and require accuracy in their work.

Wax patterns are placed in stainless steel flasks in a vacuum machine. The flasks are filled automatically with a solution called investment. This liquid, which looks like plaster of paris, is left to set hard. The flasks are then fired in a furnace at high temperature so that the wax is melted away. This is the process which gives lost wax casting its name. The casting is then placed into the casting machine and the precious metal is injected. The mould is rotated at high speed to ensure that the centrifugal force pushes the metal into the extremities of the mould. The casting is then cooled and the casting and mould separated. The **sprues** can then be broken off and the individual items separated.

See it in action . . . Margaret Turner page 10.

Some casting processes such as *shell moulding* and *die casting* have been developed specifically for **mass production.** They allow the quantity (high volume) manufacture of products. Molten metal is poured into an iron or steel die, allowed to cool and then removed.

Sand casting is not as accurate as die casting. It may provide a cheaper process for a larger product that requires minimal finishing. For example, when using an engineer's vice the surfaces that need to be 'accurate' are the contact surfaces between the fixed and sliding jaws and the screw device. The rest of the product is left 'rough cast' and finished by painting. In this situation a mechanised sand casting production line is a suitable processing method.

On the other hand the carburettor on a car is a small compact device consisting of small channels, holes and smooth surfaces. Its operational efficiency relies on its internal accuracy. In this case a form of pressure die casting may be a more suitable production method.

Whatever the method of casting or moulding, you need to consider:

● how the fluid flows through the mould,
● where to feed the fluid material into the mould,
● the fact that thin sections cool more rapidly than thick sections, and that thin sections should be fed from larger areas wherever possible.

Note also that the minimum thickness of a section depends on the material and its rate of cooling.

Finishing processes

Wood

Finishes are used to protect the wood surface from a range of effects depending on the environment where the wood will be used. French or wax polishes may be used. Spirit-based or polyurethane varnish is also available. Wood may also be protected with paint using the primer/undercoat/topcoat method or the more recently introduced one-coat finishes.

Metal

Most metals will need to be protected from corrosion in the atmosphere. Metals can be protected by covering with grease or oil (oil finishing). Metals can easily be painted with commercially available paints. Metals are often coated with plastic. This can be done in a fluidising tank. Your school will probably have one of these. Here the hot metal is dipped into a tank of fluidised plastic powder. The plastic melts on to the metal and layers of varying thickness can be built up.

Plastic

Most plastics will not need finishing but some very hard plastics may be spoilt by scratches. Scratches in plastic can be removed by using wet and dry paper of progressively finer grades, followed by abrasive polish, again using finer grades of polish.

> **See it in action . . .** Margaret Turner page 12; Wicksteed page 30; Arcam page 48; Racal Transcom page 60; President Office Furniture page 78; Naim page 91.

Corrosion proofing

> **See it in action . . .** Wicksteed page 25.

Forming

The type and physical properties of a material determine the forces needed to form it into a shape. Some metals, such as thin mild steel strip, partially spring back after bending. Steel is more resilient than copper or aluminium. The design of any bending former should reflect this property.

Timber can be steam formed, but unlike metals it has to be held under pressure for at least 24 hours.

> **See it in action . . .** Wicksteed page 30.

Bending

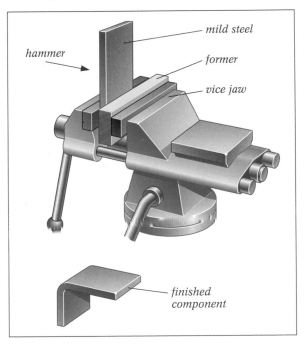

Drawing

> **See it in action . . .** Margaret Turner page 12.

◀ A vacuum former, design drawing and model formed on former.

Extrusion

Extrusion is a forming process for thermoplastics such as polyvinyl chloride (PVC) or metals such as aluminium.

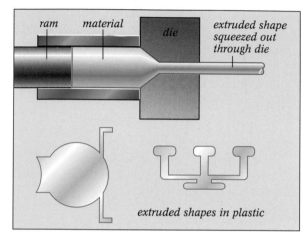

▲ *Basic extrusion technique and typical shapes produced.*

See it in action . . . Arcam page 45.

Pressing

See it in action . . . Arcam page 49.

Rolling

Hot or cold rolling techniques can produce shapes in steel. Both processes can produce simple or complex cross-sections.

Lamination

Lamination is a method to produce sheet materials and shaped sections by layering thin materials together. Wood lamination is a technique which uses layers of thin wood and synthetic adhesives. Pressure is needed to remove excess adhesive and produce the physical contact needed between the layers to provide the material strength required. The adhesive needs time to cure and harden. Heat

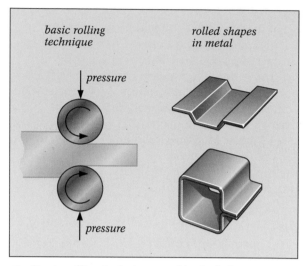

▲ *Basic rolling technique and typical shapes produced.*

may also be required to produce the curing. The former has to be designed to withstand the clamping forces and possibly heat.

See it in action . . . President Office Furniture page 77.

Machining (or wasting)

Wood

Sawing – circular saws, bandsaws, jig-saws

Planing – surface planers and thicknessers, portable planing machines (multiple point cutting tools)

Sanding – disc, bobbin and belt sanders (abrasive cutters)

Drilling – pillar and bench drills, portable power drills (multiple point cutting tools)

Turning – lathe, between centres and faceplate turning (single point tools)

Metal

Sawing – powered hacksaw, bandsaw (multiple point cutting tools)

Drilling – pillar and bench drills, portable power drills (multiple point tools)

Grinding – linlshers, off-hand/pedestal and surface grinders (abrasive cutting tools)

Turning – centre lathes, CNC lathes (single point cutting tools)

Milling – horizontal, vertical and combination CNC milling machines (multiple cutting tools)

Shaping – (single point cutting tools)

Plastics

Sawing – powered hacksaw, bandsaw (multiple point cutting tools)

Drilling – pillar and bench drills, portable power drills (multiple point tools)

Turning – centre lathes, CNC lathes (single point cutting tools)

Milling – horizontal, vertical and combination CNC milling machines (multiple cutting tools)

Shaping – (single point cutting tools)

> **See it in action** . . . Wicksteed page 26; President Office Furniture page 75.

Designing jigs, fixtures and formers

The length of a production run influences the design of **jigs** for occasional use in school workshops or your own project work.

The main design criteria below are taken into account in a cost-effective way. For example, a

drill bush for guiding drills in drilling jigs could be made out of a hardened and tempered alloy steel. A case-hardened mild steel bush may be sufficient for a small-scale production run. The design criteria for all jigs include:

- an ability to resist the forces that cutting, bending and forming generate;
- materials that possess the properties to withstand the cutting, bending and forming forces;
- a structure to resist and disperse the forces safely;
- clearly marked location points for rapid, accurate and repeatable setting;
- location that is quick, easy, secure and foolproof.

For example, a work piece should only fit one way into a drilling jig. This is particularly important for symmetrical components which can be inserted apparently correctly. Jig designers often use locating pins or inserts to ensure correct alignment of the component. If all else fails, fit a plate with either pictures or words on the jig showing the operator how to use the jig.

Design guidelines for jigs, fixtures and formers

- Keep moving or loose parts to a minimum – they are easily lost in a busy workshop.
- Work out a method for clamping components without damaging the component surface.
- Devise guides for the cutting tool.
- Think of features to ensure the safety of the operator. For example, clamping devices such as nuts and bolts should be on the operator's side of the machine where possible for ease of setting, adjusting and material removal.
- Standardise the clamping devices. For example, if using nuts and bolts, make sure they are the same size throughout – that way only one spanner will be required.
- Use quick release devices wherever possible.
- Specify a method for clearing waste material away from the cutting tool area.

You try it . . .

The circular wooden component shown below has to have six holes to accommodate six wooden dowels evenly spaced around the circumference. It is a hub section for a simple gear which is part of a wooden construction kit for young children. Consider the two designs of production drilling jig shown. Analyse the design of each by comparing how the jigs meet the design criteria outlined on page 121. Produce an evaluation of each design against the criteria, proposing modifications as appropriate.

▼ *The circular component and gear.*

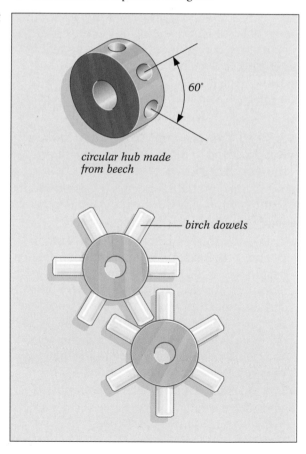

circular hub made
from beech

birch dowels

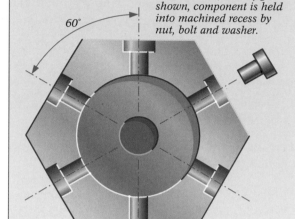

Drill bushes fit into jig as shown, component is held into machined recess by nut, bolt and washer.

60°

▲ *Drilling jig 1. The component clamps into a recessed hole in the jig and is held in place by nuts, bolts and washers. There are six individual drilling holes with hardened drill bushes. The jig, not the component, moves.*

▼ *Drilling jig 2. The component is fitted onto a cast metal body using nuts, bolts and washers. The jig has a single hardened drill bush and a locating pin set at 60° to it. This is an indexing device – after the first hole is drilled the component is swivelled so that the locating pin fits into it. The second hole is drilled and the setting up procedure is repeated.*

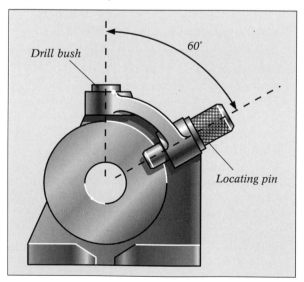

Drill bush

60°

Locating pin

Fabrication

Designers and production engineers are often faced with the problem of joining parts made out of different materials. They have to consider the relationship between service, mechanical design, product safety and specific customer requirements.

A careful choice of fabrication method has several benefits. It can speed up a production process and reduce manufacturing costs. The profitability of the product increases when the unit costs of labour, materials and equipment are reduced in relation to the agreed target selling price.

Choosing a method of fabrication

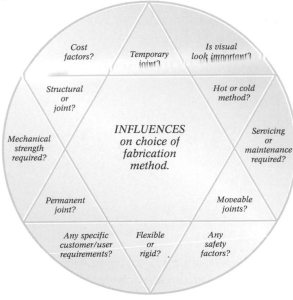

▲ *Influences on choice of fabrication methods.*

Here is a checklist based on industrial design practice. You can develop this for your own use.

Fabrication checklist

- What *volume* of products will you be producing – single items, batch or continuous flow?
- What type of *joint* do you want – permanent, temporary or a moveable joint?
- Is any *movement* required – will it be a fixed or a moving joint?
  - Do some parts have to move in a specific direction?
  - Have you analysed the movement using the principle of the six degrees of freedom?
- What types of *load* will your product be subjected to – static (fixed) or dynamic (moving)?
- Are there any *structural* considerations?
- What degree of *accuracy* is required for the product to function efficiently?
- What *mechanical properties* do you require?
- Are there any specific *functional things* you need to consider?
- Are the methods of fabrication part of the *appearance* of the product?
- Will the method of fabrication present any potential *hazards* to the users of the product?
- Do *environmental* considerations affect your choice of joining materials or fabrication?
- Do the *operating conditions or service requirements* affect your choice of fabrication (for example, vandal-proofing)?
- Will there be any *servicing or maintenance requirements* such as ease of assembly and disassembly?
- Are there any *manufacturing constraints* on you such as your skills and available resources?
- Could you use *pre-manufactured standard fastenings* – pop rivets, nuts, bolts, screws, knock-down (KD) fittings?

Mechanical jointing

The greatest part of assembly costs is labour. Jointing by mechanical fasteners – nuts, bolts, studs, screws and spring fasteners – gives a designer a chance to reduce overall costs.

Mechanical fasteners

Mechanical fasteners include self-tapping screws, rivets, nuts and bolts and many other specialist devices.

Nuts and bolts

Nuts and bolts are used where a temporary joint is needed. Nuts and bolts may be used to give a fixed or a moving joint.

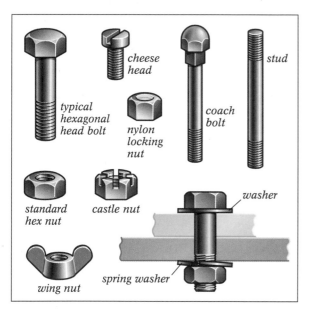

▲ Nuts and bolts.

There are different types of bolts:

- cheese-head bolt – used as a temporary fixing;
- hexagonal-head bolt – bolting steel parts together;
- coach bolt – these are used to join beams together;
- stud bolt – these are used to clamp materials together; a nut must be placed at both ends of this bolt.

The type of nut placed on the end can also vary. These may be 'nylok' nuts, wing nuts, castle nuts or hexagonal nuts.

Washers distribute clamping forces evenly through the joint.

Self-tapping screws

Self-tapping screws are used to fasten thin sheet metal together or fittings to sheet metal.

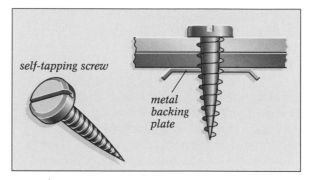

▲ Using a self-tapping screw.

See it in action ... Racal Transcom page 59.

Mechanical fastener checklist

When you need to decide whether or not to use mechanical fasteners you need to consider these questions.

- What properties are required?
- What forces will be acting on the fabricated parts?
- How can dissimilar materials be joined (for example, metal to wood, plastic to metal)?
- How may corrosion between dissimilar metals (for example, steel rivets in aluminium) be avoided?

Mechanical jointing in wood-based products

Modern furniture is generally made using composite materials. Modern marketing techniques like flat-pack and self-assembly furniture have produced many new joining techniques. This has led to a major new industry producing **knock-down (KD) fittings** and specialist fastening devices which are designed to allow non-specialists to construct products such as wardrobes, tables and chairs.

The effectiveness of the process relies on the manufacturer's ability to 'design out' the fabrication problems.

- Holes for screw fittings are pre-drilled.
- The fixing screw may not be the traditional type but be specially designed for screwing into **composite** materials.

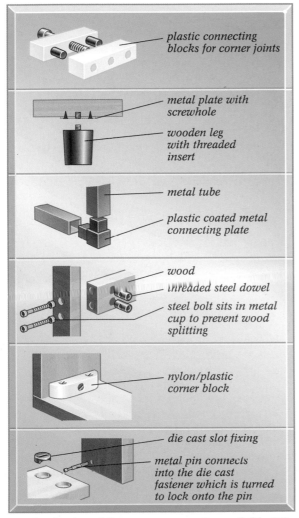

▲ *A selection of the more commonly available KD fittings and fastenings for wood-based products.*

- Doors are supplied with two sets of fixing holes for hinges which allows doors to open to the left or the right, so one door has two opening options.
- Shelves in cupboards can be fixed at different heights by providing a number of pre-drilled holes and plastic plugs.
- Cabinets supplied without backs can fit directly to the wall using dual-purpose metal corner brackets. Apart from fixing the cabinet to the wall, the brackets provide corner joints that help to resist the loads imparted by the cabinet and its contents.

> **You try it ...**
>
> Investigate applying these components and technologies to improve the quality of your own products. A visit to a local ironmonger or DIY store will give you an idea of the fabrication products that are available. Several manufacturers and large warehouses publish catalogues which will help you to start your own design library. This technique of analysing how products are designed, manufactured, fabricated and costed is known in industry as **reverse engineering** and is a vital skill.

Mechanical fasteners for metal

The choice of mechanical fastener for metal depends on:

- operating and service conditions – heat, humidity and pressure;
- physical characteristics required in the joint – for example, elasticity or corrosion resistance;
- nature of load on the joint – for example, shear, tensile (pulling), torsional (twisting), cyclic (repeated regularly), impact, vibrational;
- type of manufacturing assembly – hand or automatic machine based;
- access required to joint for servicing or maintenance purposes;
- target cost for the assembly.

Spring steel fasteners can be used to put metal components together quickly and economically.

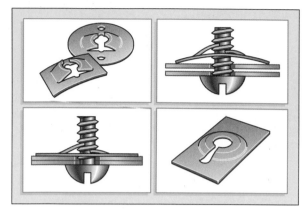

▲ Spring steel fasteners for threaded screws, plate or flat nuts. The spring in the steel acts as a thread lock on the root of the self-tapping fixing screw. The spring lock prevents the joint vibrating loose.

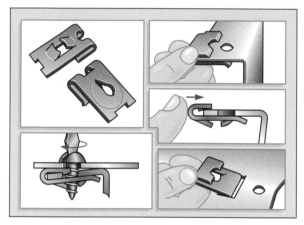

▲ Variations on the plate nut – the 'J' nut.

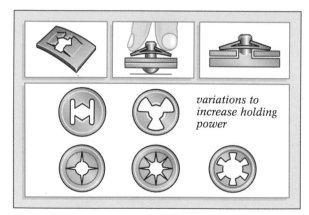

variations to increase holding power

▲ Spring steel fasteners for unthreaded bars – 'push-on' fixings used on products such as children's toys (fixing wheels onto axles, decorative trim inside cars).

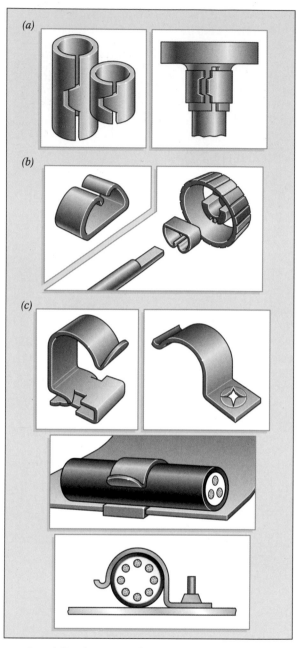

(a)

(b)

(c)

▲ Specialist fastening devices using spring steel fixings: (a) compression rings for fixing thermoplastic fittings to axles or spindles; (b) clips for securing plastic control knobs to electrical or mechanical products – they are easily pulled off to allow removal of control panels; (c) cable clips, either fixed or self-retaining.

See it in action … Arcam page 49; Racal Transcom page 59.

Thermal fabrication

Thermal fabrication makes permanent joints between two metals using heat and an alloy that has a lower melting point than the metals being joined. The higher the temperature, the greater the strength of the joint. The strength also depends on the filler alloys used as well as the chemical and physical factors outlined below.

Filler alloys
- Soft solders – tin/lead, 180–230 °C
- Hard solders – silver/copper/zinc, 625–750 °C
- Brazing – copper/zinc, 850 °C
- Welding – same as 'parent' metals

Chemical factors
All metals react with oxygen in the air when heated – they oxidise. The use of a *flux* prevents this. There are two main types to consider:

- passive, resin- or borax-based fluxes – these work by excluding air and by chemically preventing oxide formation;
- active, acid-based fluxes, such as zinc chloride – these chemically clean a joint as well as exclude air from a joint; joints need washing at the end of the process to remove acid residues.

Physical factors
These include:

- type of joint;
- size of joint area;
- distribution of heat through the joint (this must be even).

▼ *Types of thermal joint.*

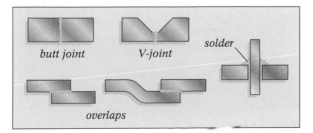

butt joint   V-joint   solder

overlaps

Soldering

See it in action ... Margaret Turner page 12; Naim page 88.

Welding
There is a wide range of welding processes which use a variety of energy sources. Welding often involves the use of burning gases (for example, oxyacetylene) or electric arcs.

In **fusion welding** the materials are heated until they melt and fuse together. Fusion welding provides strong joints in steel but the joints are not as malleable or corrosion resistant as joints that are bronze welded. In any application where there is likely to be regular flexing of materials or severe environmental conditions you might consider using bronze welding.

Bronze welding is a similar process to soldering and brazing – the materials being joined do not melt. They are fluxed, heated and then a brass or bronze filler rod is melted to form a physical joint between the parts.

The cost of bronze or brass filler rods is much greater than steel welding rods. In certain situations, providing the joint is not too large, such as those on bicycle and kart frames, bronze welding is used in preference to fusion welding.

Bronze welding is often preferred to oxyacetylene welding in school because less heat is required. A flux is needed. Larger gaps can be filled using bronze welding than using brazing or soldering.

See it in action ... Wicksteed page 27.

Adhesives

An adhesive is a material which is capable of bonding (holding) two surfaces together in a strong, often permanent, joint. Until the 1940s natural adhesives, usually referred to as glues, were in everyday use. Natural glues are animal- or vegetable-based and include gelatine made from bones, animal hide, fish, and a range of vegetable-based gums. They are still used for specialist applications like antique furniture restoration or for sticking paper and similar materials. As the modern plastics industry has grown, glues have been gradually replaced or modified by synthetic (manufactured) adhesives.

Adhesives can be classified in a number of ways:

- natural or synthetic;
- reaction to heat (**thermoplastic** and **thermosetting** adhesives);
- ability to remain rigid or to stretch (elastomer adhesives);
- ability to withstand environmental conditions, for example moisture resistance affects interior or exterior use;
- in terms of fabrication time, for example cold and hot setting.

Synthetic adhesives

Most synthetic adhesives are polymer materials that have strength and flexibility. Thermoplastic resin adhesives, such as vinyl resins and cellulose derivatives, can be softened by heating.

The most common uses are the bonding of wood, rubber, metal, and paper products. Some thermoplastics, such as the polyamides (nylons), polyethylene, and polyvinyl acetate (PVA), are used as hot-melt adhesives in electrically heated glue guns. The adhesive is applied in molten state to form a rigid bond on cooling.

Thermosetting adhesives

Thermosetting adhesives, which include a large number of synthetic resins, are converted by the use of heat or a chemical catalyst and, sometimes, pressure into insoluble (moisture resistant) and rigid materials. Household **epoxy resin** adhesives are supplied in component form as two separate tubes of chemical, one tube contains the resin, the other a curing agent (hardener). The two chemicals are mixed just before application. The mix soon sets hard, usually at room temperature. Epoxy resins may be expensive to buy in small quantities but they provide tough, strong joints that shrink very little as they harden. In an industrial situation the mixing of the two parts is accurately controlled using a specially designed 'gun' which mixes the parts. The gun is supplied from separate dispensers.

▲ *Glue gun in use.*

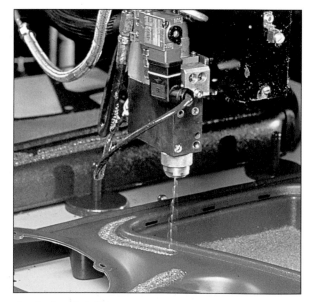

▲ *Industrial dispenser.*

Elastomeric adhesives

Elastomeric (stretching) adhesives include natural and synthetic rubber cements and are used for bonding flexible materials such as synthetic rubber, paper, textiles and leather or to provide flexible joints in more resistant materials. Superglues are fast-setting cyanoacrylate adhesives which are used in very small quantities.

Joint design and adhesives

Synthetic adhesives are often stronger than the materials they are joining. The design of jointing systems has changed. When the only materials available for furniture were soft and hard woods such as pine and oak, designers not only thought about how the joint would look, they designed joints as mechanical structures.

A joint is designed, shaped and formed to achieve the required mechanical properties such as shear strength or stiffness. Compare the triangular shape and design of the dovetail joint with the parallel sides of the comb joint shown. One joint is ideally suited to be load bearing and resist pulling forces, the other would seem to be easier to pull apart.

The modern mass production furniture industry uses power-driven tools so joints have to be easily machinable. Finger joints fixed using a synthetic resin may now meet the mass production design criteria of strength, rigidity, machinability and reduced manufacturing time. The dovetail joint may be more labour intensive and so more costly to produce. It may even be over-designed because it can resist much greater forces than the joint may ever be subjected to.

Natural adhesives are generally made from non-toxic substances and present few hazards in use. Synthetic adhesives can contain

Advantages and disadvantages of adhesive bonding.

Advantages
- Weight and cost are often lower than using a mechanical joint.
- The materials are not weakened by drilling fixing holes.
- Smooth profiles and a fluid seal significantly reduce the risk of corrosion.
- Thin sheets of material can be joined effectively without the distorting effects of heat or pressure.
- The adhesive can act as an insulator and reduce the electro-chemical corrosion caused when two dissimilar metals are in contact with each other.

Disadvantages
- The shear strength of adhesives is much lower than that of mechanical methods of jointing.
- Joints cannot be disassembled.
- Adhesive joints can be severely affected by small extremes of temperature.
- The surface finish of materials affects the overall strength of an adhesive joint.
- The insulating effects of an adhesive may be unacceptable.

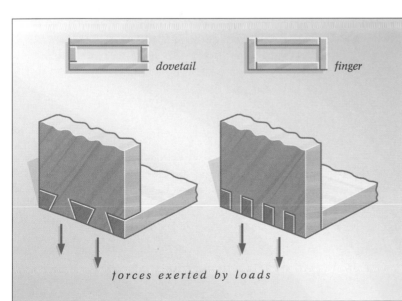

forces exerted by loads

◀ Dovetail and finger comb joints, showing the forces on them. Which joint is more likely to pull apart?

Summary chart of common adhesives.		
Type	**Curing method**	**Typical uses**
Plastic cements	Chemical – solvent based	Solvent-based cements available for Acrylic, PVC, rigid polystyrene.
Modified phenolic resins	Thermosetting – heat and pressure	Metal-metal, metal-wood, wood, metal and plastic joints. Used in laminating and high load situations. Joints are waterproof but leave clearly visible brown glue lines.
Epoxy-based adhesives	Chemical – hardening compound reacting with resin, sometimes heat	Preparation is critical, most materials can be joined.
Polyurethane adhesives	Chemical – reaction between two substances	Anywhere a fast-acting joint is required.
Rubber-based adhesives	Solvent base that evaporates	Contact or impact – fixing dissimilar materials, for example, plastic laminates to manufactured boards. No pressure needed, joints not strong, short shelf life once opened.
PVA adhesives	Thermoplastic water-based emulsion, removal of water	Commonly used, white ready mixed liquid for bonding porous materials such as wood. A non-staining adhesive that is not waterproof.
Hot melts	Thermosetting – heat	Quick joints in any situation where there are light loads.

substances requiring careful use. The way substances can be used are outlined in **COSHH** regulations which should be available in any workplace which uses chemicals and hazardous substances. Manufacturers are always expected to supply a COSHH statement with their product.

Safety first

Work in well-ventilated areas and wear appropriate protective equipment. Do not use any substance without consulting either your teacher or the **Hazcard** for the product. If no Hazcard is available do not use the substance.

▼ *Cyanoacrylate safety data sheet from Loctite.*

Loctite International
NBD – Health & Regulatory Affairs

SAFETY DATA SHEET

This safety data sheet has been prepared in accordance with the requirements of EC Directive 88/379/EEC and 91/155/EEC (and other related directives) and provides information relating to the safe handling and use of the product.

Date: 5th January 1994

1. PRODUCT IDENTIFICATION

1.1. Product Name: *Superglue 3*

1.2. Company Name:
Manufacturer: LOCTITE (Ireland) Limited
Local Distributor: LOCTITE UK

1.3. Emergency Contact (24 Hour Service):
First Call Local Distributor: Tel:–   0707 821000
Contact Name: HEALTH & SAFETY OFFICER

Manufacturer: Tel: +353-1-510433 or +353-1-519466, Fax: +353-1-519073

2. COMPOSITIONAL INFORMATION

Nature: Cyanoacrylate adhesive

Component	% bv Wt*	Hazard Class
Ethylcyanoacrylate	95.0	–
Polyalkylmethacrylate	6.0	–
Stabilizers	0.1	–

(percentages are less than those given.)

3. HAZARDS IDENTIFICATION
Bonds skin and eyes in seconds. Highly reactive to water. (See Section 4 on First aid)

4. FIRST AID MEASURES

Inhalation:
Remove affected person to fresh air.

Skin Contact:
Do not pull bonded skin apart. It may be gently peeled apart using a blunt object such as a spoon, preferably after soaking in warm soapy water.

Eye Contact:
If the eye is bonded closed, release eyelashes with warm water by covering with wet pad. Cyanoacrylate will bond to eye protein causing lacrymatory effect which will help to debond adhesive. Keep eye covered with wet pad until debonding is complete, usually within 1–3 days. Do not force eye open. Medical advice should be sought in case solid particles of cyanoacrylate trapped behind the eyelid cause any abrasive damage.

Ingestion:
Ensure that breathing passages are not obstructed. The product will polymerise immediately in the mouth making it almost impossible to swallow. Saliva will slowly separate the solidified product from the mouth (several hours).

5. FIRE FIGHTING MEASURES

Non flammable product (flash point is greater than 80°C (CC)).
If product is involved in fire extinguish with dry powder, foam or carbon dioxide. Trace amounts of toxic fumes may be released on incineration and the use of breathing apparatus is recommended.

6. ACCIDENTAL RELEASE MEASURES

Ventilate area. Do not use cloths for mopping up. Polymerise with water and scrape off floor.

7. HANDLING & STORAGE

7.1. Handling:
Ventilation (low level) is recommended when using large volumes or where odour becomes apparent (odour threshold value is approximately 1–2ppm).
Use of dispensing equipment is recommended to minimise the risk of skin or eye contact.

7.2. Storage:
Store in original containers at 5°C–28°C and do not return residual materials to containers as contamination may reduce the shelf life of the bulk product.

8. EXPOSURE CONTROLS – PERSONAL PROTECTION

Polyethylene or polypropylene gloves are recommended when using large volumes. Do not use PVC, rubber or nylon gloves. Eye protection should be used where there is any risk of splashing.
The TLV for the closely related methyl cyanoacrylate is 2ppm (ACGIH, TWA).

9. PHYSICAL & CHEMICAL PROPERTIES
Appearance: *Clear liquid*
Odour: Sharp characteristic
pH: Not applicable

(The following properties are to be interpreted within the meaning of Directive 67/548/EEC)

Boiling point: >100°C
Flash Point (Closed cup): >80°C
Specific Gravity: Approx. 1.1g/ml @ 20°C
Solubility in Water: Immiscible (rapidly polymerised by water).
Solubility in Chloroform: NA
Vapour Pressure: <0.5 mmHg @ 25°C
Other Properties: NA

10. STABILITY & REACTIVITY
Polymerisation will occur in the presence of moisture.

11. TOXICOLOGICAL INFORMATION

Inhalation:
In dry atmosphere with <50% relative humidity, vapours may irritate the eyes and respiratory system.
Prolonged exposure to high concentrations of vapours may lead to chronic effects in sensitive individuals.

Skin:
Bonds skin in seconds. Considered to be of low toxicity; Acute dermal LD50 (rabbit) >2000mg/kg. Due to polymerisation at the skin surface allergic reaction is not considered possible.

Eye:
Liquid product will bond eyelids. In a dry atmosphere (RH<50%) vapours may cause irritation and lachrymatory effect.

Ingestion:
Cyanoacrylates are considered to have relatively low toxicity. Acute oral LD50 is >5000mg/kg (rat). It is almost impossible to swallow as it rapidly polymerises in the mouth.

12. ECOLOGICAL INFORMATION
Biodegradable product of low ecotoxicity. Does not contain and is not manufactured with any of the substances listed on the Montreal protocol.

13. DISPOSAL
Polymerise by adding slowly to water (10:1). Dispose of as water insoluble non-toxic solid chemicals in authorised landfill or incinerate under controlled conditions.
Dispose of in accordance with local and national regulations.

14. TRANSPORT INFORMATION

UN No.: 1993 (For ADR/RID only)
Air(IATA): Not classified.
Sea(IMO): Not classified.
Road/Rail (ADR/RID): Inflammable liquid. Class 3, label No. 3, Item No 32(c).

15. REGULATORY INFORMATION
Hazard Label:

Cyanoacrylate.
Danger.
Bonds skin in seconds.
Keep out of the reach of children

Risk Phrases: None

Safety Phrases: None

16. OTHER INFORMATION
Further information may be obtained from the Health & Regulatory Affairs Department at the following address:-

Loctite (International) NBD
Tallaght Business Park,
Whitestown,
Dublin 24, Ireland.
Tel: +353-1-510433 or +353-1-519466.
Fax: +353-1-519073

Prepared by:

Susan Lennox, MSc.,
Health & Regulatory Affairs Officer.

Internal Formula Ref.: EG 408 82/09 HRA Ref.: –
Formerly Development Product: –
Supercedes Safety Data Sheet No: –
Our ref. SL/MC

The information in this safety data sheet was obtained from reputable sources and to the best of our knowledge, is accurate and current at the mentioned date. Neither Loctite nor its subsidiary companies accept any liability arising out of the use of the information provided here or the use, application or processing of the product(s) described herein. Attention of users is drawn to the possible hazards from improper use of the product(s).

	Wood	Metal	Acrylic	Expanded polystyrene	Melamine	Polystyrene	Fabric	Rubber	Leather
Wood	PVA or synthetic resin								
Metal	epoxy resin								
Acrylic	epoxy resin		acrylic cement						
Expanded polystyrene	PVA								
Melamine	contact adhesive								
Polystyrene	contact adhesive					Polystyrene cement			
Fabric	PVA or contact	contact adhesive					PVA or latex		
Rubber	contact adhesive or latex adhesive							rubber solution	
Leather	contact adhesive or epoxy resin								
Material	Wood	Metal	Acrylic	Expanded polystyrene	Melamine	Polystyrene	Fabric	Rubber	Leather

▲ Matching adhesives to the material being joined.

Glossary

ABS plastic (acrylonitrile-butadiene-styrene)
A plastic made from a mixture of acrylic (hard, high lustre surface), butadiene (rubber) and styrene (rigid, high impact strength). Each of the three materials contributes to the characteristics of ABS. It is opaque, fairly stiff, hard and easy to cut, and leaves a smooth edge when cut. It is commonly used for casings of household appliances.

amorphous
Materials in which the atoms or molecules have no definite pattern.

amplifier
A circuit which will increase the strength of a signal.

analogue signal
A signal that can vary continuously between a maximum and minimum value.

anthropometric data
This is measurement information collected about the range of sizes of people. It may contain data about heights, arm lengths, feet sizes, hand spans, etc. The data is used to help designers to produce products or environments which are suitable for the majority of people.

anneal
Heat metal and allow it to cool gradually which removes stresses and hardness from the metal.

batch production
The oldest form of factory organisation, where a wide variety of components or products are made in small quantities. It is still the major manufacturing system in use today because of the need for the supply of a large variety of parts, components and products in relatively small quantities.

bi-metallic corrosion
Corrosion that occurs when two dissimilar materials, such as copper and cast iron, are connected together. In the presence of a suitable electrolyte, such as water, an electrochemical cell (a major corrosion mechanism) is set up between the two metals.

bit
Binary digIT used to represent digits 0 or 1 in the binary system.

CAD
Computer-aided design – a term which describes computer work in three areas: drawing (draughting), solid (three-dimensional) modelling, and mathematical modelling.

CAD/CAM
Computer-aided design/computer-aided manufacture – a design and production process employing computerised manufacturing systems and controls

CAE
Computer-aided engineering – a general term describing the use of computer techniques in manufacturing industry.

casting methods
Ways of producing a cast or moulded shape.

CIM, CNC
Computer-integrated manufacture (CIM) is a manufacturing philosophy in which computers are used directly in manufacturing operations. CNC (computer numerically controlled) machines are directly controlled by numbers from a computer processor which require highly skilled personnel to set them up.

composite

Two or more materials are combined to obtain different properties than those available in the original materials. Concrete, plywood and glass reinforced polyester (GRP) are known as composite materials.

computer library

An electronic file that carries pre-drawn information and saves design and drawing time.

component standardisation

Using a component in more than one product.

concurrent engineering

A method of developing and manufacturing products that uses a team-based approach to project management and continuous improvement. Also known as **simultaneous engineering**.

configuring

Shaping or arranging.

corporate

Belonging to or pertaining to a corporation or company.

COSHH

Control of substances hazardous to health.

critical control points

During any manufacturing process there are specific points at which a product or process must be checked to ensure that the finished product will meet specification and service requirements. These occur at the critical control points and are monitored by a quality control system which makes go/no go (yes/no) decisions. A product cannot 'go' to the next stage of manufacture without meeting the specified quality indicator at the designated critical control point.

crystalline

A substance that has an organised structure. The atoms or molecules are joined together to form definite regular patterns. All metals are crystalline.

database

A large collection of related information (data) on a particular topic such as materials or anthropometric data.

desktop manufacturing

A technique that integrates design and manufacturing. It allows designers to model and make plastic prototypes directly from the computer. This enables them to think about manufacture at an earlier stage when designs are easy to change. Large companies can save huge amounts of money in development costs alone.

digital signal

A signal having one of two values – on or off, high or low, 1 or 0.

dimensional co-ordination

Design system using standard anthropometric data.

downloading

Loading electronic data and information from a storage system such as disks, a host computer or computer library. Electronic information is often transferred by internal computer networks or an external modem on a telephone line.

drawing plate

A metal plate which has holes of various sizes. Annealed silver or copper wire is pulled through the holes to reduce the diameter of the wire.

EFTPOS

Electronic funds transfer at point of sale.

electrochemical cell

A small battery can be formed between two components of dissimilar material. It requires a fluid to conduct the current flow. The component which is highest up the electrochemical series forms the anode which gives up its electrons (dissolves, corrodes) to the cathode which can receive them. A typical example of electrochemical corrosion would be to join aluminium using steel screws in a damp environment.

environmental impact

An indication of the local, regional or global environmental consequences of a process or activity.

epoxy resin
Synthetic polymers which, when mixed together, form a strong adhesive bond. Such adhesives are frequently used to join dissimilar materials and are normally purchased as two separate tubes, an adhesive and a hardener.

ergonomic
Suitable for use by humans. An ergonomic product is designed for maximum safety, comfort, health and efficiency.

extrusion
A shape that is achieved by forcing suitable materials through a die by means of a ram.

fettle
To knock or rub excess material off the edges – usually relates to a casting.

FMS (flexible manufacturing systems)
Flexible manufacturing systems do not rely totally on computers. A company may organise their workforce into 'production cells' which is a team approach so that an operation is not totally dependent on one person. Computers may be limited to use in key target areas such as material handling or progress chasing.

Four Ps
See **marketing, marketing mix**

fusion welding
In fusion welding the materials are heated until they melt and fuse together. This limits its use to metals and thermoplastics.

Hazcard
Description of the potential health and safety hazards associated with the use of substances in the workplace.

host computers
A computer attached to and in control of a multi-terminal computer system, or one attached to a multi-computer network and able to provide access to a number of databases.

injection units
These units are used for forcing plastic material through a mould or die.

interface
Either the hardware that allows different devices to be connected to a computer or an electronic device like a relay that allows a low voltage circuit to control high voltage equipment.

jig
An appliance for guiding or positioning a tool or appliance for use in mechanical processes.

knock-down fitting (KD)
A pre-manufactured component used to make quick assembly joints between similar or dissimilar materials.

lamination, laminates
A method of producing sheet materials or shaped sections by layering thin materials together. The layers are joined using a suitable adhesive or bonding agent, sometimes under the action of heat and pressure.

logo
A design used as a symbol of an organisation.

logotype
A design incorporating symbols and letters.

manufacturability
The ability of components or products to be manufactured usually from available resources, hence design for manufacturability.

market
A market includes all the buyers and sellers of particular products and services. Traditionally markets were geographical areas where people met to make contact and exchange goods and money. Now markets vary in size, location and specialism. For example, the London Stock Exchange is a market made up of thousands of individuals and companies, professionals and non-professionals who never meet but who still complete millions of pounds worth of business each day. Another example is the area around Tottenham Court Road in London where there is a concentration of dealers specialising in selling electrical and electronic goods. Prices are very competitive and the area attracts vast numbers of customers.

market research

This is the process by which information about a market is collected to inform company decision making.

marketing, marketing mix

Marketing is a process which aims to make existing products and services attractive to potential buyers. It can also create the demand for a new product. There are four key elements to marketing, known as the **Four Ps**:

Product – what are the features of the product or service?

Price – what factors affect how the product should be priced?

Place – where will the product be sold?

Promotion – what methods will be used to promote the product?

The *marketing mix* is the way these elements are combined to meet the needs of different customer groupings. In some cases a target group is defined at the outset of a project. Grouping could be by age, gender, income or salary level, religion or combinations of other factors.

mass production

The manufacture of large numbers of parts and components that are identical in size and configuration. It also describes the assembly of large numbers of identical finished products made from the previously produced components and parts.

milestone

A key point in a project management process which indicates the completion of a particular operation or process.

modem

Modulator-**dem**odulator. An electronic device used to transmit and receive data as frequency-modulated tone over a communications system.

PCB

Printed circuit board.

piece part

A single item.

planishing hammer

A hammer used to shape and polish metal. The hammer surfaces are highly polished.

plasticising

Adding a chemical to a plastic to make it more pliable, softer, and easier to mould or shape.

prototype

The final part of a design development process, the prototype is made to work and resemble the finished product as closely as possible.

quality assurance

The activities planned to ensure that a product or service will satisfy the requirements for quality. It takes place throughout the process.

quality control

The procedures for inspecting products and detecting those that are not up to standard.

quality indicator

An essential part of any quality assurance system – a written statement that sets acceptable limits or standards for a component or product.

reverse engineering

A design technique to deconstruct existing products to establish methods of manufacture, key design features and materials used.

sequential engineering

A system that relies on a linear sequencing of design and manufacturing activities; work in progress is passed through a series of discrete self-contained stages.

In this, the designer passes onto a production engineer who decides how it will or will not be made. If the design cannot be manufactured it is passed back to the designer. This passing back and forth 'over the wall' can happen at any stage from idea to market. It is time consuming and an inefficient use of resources. When the product goes on sale, it may sell or it may not. By this stage it may have become a very expensive mistake!

simultaneous engineering

A method of developing and manufacturing products that uses a team-based approach to project management and continuous

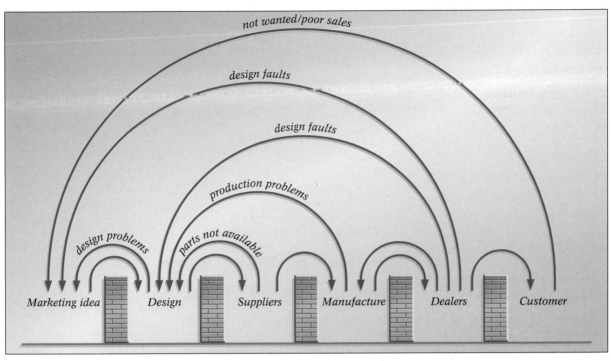

▲ *Sequential engineering; also known as the 'over the wall' approach.*

improvement. Also known as **concurrent engineering**. Contrast this with **sequential engineering**.

solid modelling
A computer-based technique that represents the solid nature of an object and not just its external appearance. The designer builds up complex parts by combining basic shapes, such as boxes, cylinders, spheres and cones. It provides realistic shaded images of the model in various positions. The computer also calculates properties such as weight, volume, location of the centre of gravity and surface area automatically.

specification
The particular requirements. A detailed description.

sprue
A passage by which molten metals run into a mould. The metal that solidifies in it.

template
A mould cut to the required outline to use as a guide for producing similar parts.

thermal shock
Stress which very often results in a fracture when an object is subjected to sudden changes in temperature.

thermoplastic
A plastic that will soften when heated and harden when cooled. This process is repeatable and can be compared to the melting and resolidifying of a familiar material such as candle wax.

thermoset
A plastic that solidifies on heating and cannot be reformed.

uploading
Sending data or information to a device such as a computerised milling machine.

vulcanised
Treated with sulphur at a high temperature.

work-hardened
Bent and pressed so that the internal structure of the metal changes to make it stronger and harder.

Index

ABS plastic 60, 62, 114, 117, 135
acetate 115
acrylic 115, 134
acrylonitrile 116
adhesives 127–30, 134
advertising 7–8, 74; *see also* marketing
aesthetics in design 44
Allen keys 33
alloys 51, 113, 127
Alpha One CD player 38, 40–4, 47–50
aluminium 91
amplifiers 45–7
annealing 12
anodising 91
anthropometric data 79, 94–6, 106–7, 135
Arcam
    Alpha amplifier 45–7
    Alpha One CD 38, 40–4, 47–50
    management structure 36
    marketing 36–9, 54
    product range 38–9
    production 50–3
automatic test equipment 51

batch production 10–11, 85
bending 29–30, 119
block model 108, 110
bolts 124
brand image 48
brand loyalty 38
brazing 127
British Standards Institute 15, 93
    BS 4778 99
    BS 5696 15, 20
    BS 5750 15, 100
buffing 12
business plans 7
butt joint 27, 28

CAD 103–7, 135
    for advertising 7
    PCBs 87
    for play equipment 34
CAD/CAM systems 60, 105–7, 135
carbon fibre reinforced plastics 117
Cardmate 2 57–63
casting 10, 117, 118, 135
CD players 38, 40–4, 47–50
cellulose acetate 115
chassis 47–50, 59, 60, 62
chemicals, health and safety 130
chipboard 75, 113–14
CIM 107
clamping device 31, 121
CNC machine 48–9, 87, 135
commissions 7
company image 7–8
components 26, 27
    assembly of 32–5, 62
    manufacture of 11, 25–7
    for PCBs 88
    standardisation of 48, 136
composites 113–14, 136
compression rings 126
computer numerically controlled machine: *see* CNC
computer system, block diagram 104
computer-aided design: *see* CAD
computer-controlled multiple tool manufacturing 30
computer-integrated manufacture: *see* CIM
concurrent engineering 40–4, 101, 136
continuous improvement 101
copolymers 114
copper 87
corporate image 91, 92
corrosion 25–6, 119

COSHH, adhesives 130, 136
costs 45, 47, 98
Critical Fall Height 23
crystal lattice structures 112

data analysis, research 97
design
    aesthetics 44
    anthropometrics 94–6
    CAD 7, 34, 87, 103–7, 135
    and costs 45, 47, 98
    EFTPOS 57–8
    fabrication checklist 123
    hi-fi 40–2, 82–5
    jewellery 9–10
    of jigs, fixtures and formers 121–2
    modification 62
    office furniture 65–70
    for playground systems 17–19
    quality in 100–1
    resources for 9
    specification 64
    standards 44
design briefs 40–4, 58, 71–3, 93, 94
Design Clinic 74
design-manufacturing product development 73
desktop manufacturing 105, 136
dimensional co-ordination 18, 78–9, 106–7, 136
directed assembly equipment 50
downloading 107
drafting programs, automated 104
drawing plate 12, 136
drilling 28, 29, 120, 121–2

edging 77
EFTPOS (electronic funds transfer at point of sale) 56–8

elastomeric adhesives 129
elastomers 114, 116–17
electronics design 44
environmental impact 19, 24, 74, 136
epoxide 116
epoxy resin 84, 87, 116, 128, 130, 137
ergonomics 20–1, 59, 69, 94–6, 108, 137
European Safety Standards 17
extrusion 91, 120, 137

fabrication 45, 123
    jewellery 12–13
    requirements 111
    thermal 27–8, 127
fettling 11, 137
fibreglass-reinforced polyester 117
finishing processes 117, 118–19
fittings 33, 125, 137
fixtures 28, 30–32, 121–2
flange 50
flat packs 48, 78–9, 124–5
flux 12, 13, 88, 89, 127
FM Design 71, 72–3
foams 114, 117
formaldehydes 116
formers 28, 30–32, 121–2
forming 117, 119–20

glue guns 128
glues 127–8, 129
graphics system, object-oriented 104
grinding 121
GRP 117

hallmarking 13
Hazcards 130
hi-fi 36–9, 54, 80, 81
    amplifiers 45–7
    CD players 38, 40–4, 47–50
    loudspeakers 82–5
hinges 31
hot melt adhesives 130
hot-desking 68

information technology 66
injection moulding 60, 62, 77, 118
integrated circuits 88
interlock 27

ISO 9000 100

jewellery 6
    designing 9–10
    fabrication 12–13
    marketing 7–8
    production 10–11
jigs
    for bending 29–30
    for drilling 28, 29, 121–2
    in PCBs 87
    for welding 30
joining
    metal 27–8, 125–6
    wood 124–6, 129
joints
    adhesives 127–30
    mechanical 124–6
    thermal 127
    welded 27–8, 127

Kanban manufacturing system 86
kitchen furniture 94, 106–7
knock-down fittings 125, 137
Kyo range 65, 66, 68–71, 74

laminating 75, 117, 120
life cycle assessment 24
line production 51, 52
logo 7, 65, 74, 91–2
lost wax casting 10–11, 118
loudspeakers 82–5

machining 117, 120–1
malleability 112
manufacturing
    computer-controlled
        multiple tool 30
    desktop 105, 136
    Kanban system 86
    material requirements 111
    quality indicators 74, 99
    specifications 99
manufacturing defects analyser 51
market research 36–7, 48, 97–8
marketing 101, 138
    hi-fi 36–9, 54
    jewellery 7–8
    Kyo 74
    office furniture 65, 66–8
    Wicksteed Leisure Ltd 14–15

mass production 118, 138
materials
    for manufacture 75–8
    physical and mechanical properties 111–12
    processing 117–22
    resistant 111
MDF (medium density fibreboard) 75, 85
mechanical design 44
mechanical fasteners 124–6
mechanisms, and movement 31–2
melamine 75
melamine-formaldehyde 116
metals 112–13
    adhesives for 134
    finishes 119
    forming 119
    machining 121
    mechanical fasteners 125–6
milestone plan, concurrent engineering 43, 138
milling 121
models 73, 103–4, 108–10
modem 58, 138
modules 17–18, 72
moulding 10–11, 60, 62, 114, 117, 118
movement, freedom of 31–2

Naim Audio Limited 80, 82–6, 91, 92
nuts 101, 126
nylon 115

object-oriented graphics system 104
office furniture 65, 66–71, 74, 77, 78

paint 25, 91, 118
panels, surface finishes 48
PCBs 46, 50–3, 87–91
peening 32, 33
percentiles 94, 95
phenol-formaldehyde 116
phenolic resins, modified 130
photo-electric cell detector 75
piece part costs 49
planing 120
planishing hammer 12, 138
plastic cements 130
plasticising 60

plastics 77, 114–17, 119, 121, 135
play equipment 15–16, 17–19
    CAD 34
    component manufacture 25–8
    ergonomics 20–1
    fastenings 32–5
    modules 17–18
    safety features 18, 21–4
plywood 113–14
polishing 12, 118
polyamide (nylon) 115
polycarbonate 116
polyester resin 116
polyethene 115
polyethylene 115
polymers 114, 117, 128
polymethyl methacrylate 115
polypropylene 116
polystyrene 114, 115, 117, 134
polyurethane adhesives 130
polyvinyl acetate (PVA) 130
polyvinyl chloride (PVC) 115, 117
President Office Furniture 65–71
press tool 48
printed circuit board: see PCB
product development 40–4
    anthropometric data 94–6
    CAD/CAM systems 103–7
    compatibility 80
    design 44–5, 73
    market research 97–8
    quality 98–103
    specification 93–4
product matrix 38–9
product reviews 54, 103
production 51–3
    batch 10–11, 85
    cell 51
    line 51, 52
    mass 118, 138
project management 138–9; see also simultaneous engineering
prototype 43–4, 71–3, 93, 109, 110

quality 98–103
quality action teams 101
quality assurance 26, 31, 93, 99, 138
quality control 99, 100, 138

quality indicators 74, 99, 138
questionnaire design 97

Racal Transcom 56–63
recycling 24
research 97; see also market research
reverse engineering 125, 138
reviews 54, 103
rolling 120
roundabouts 21, 22
routing machine 76
rubber 10–11, 117, 134, 139
rubber based adhesives 130

safety
    adhesive data sheet 131–4
    Hazcards 130
    play equipment 21–4
    routing machine 76, 77
    wax modelling 10
    welding 28
Safety of Toys (BSEN 71) 17
sanding 120
sawing 120, 121
screws 31, 32, 33, 124
see-saws 21, 22
sequential engineering 40–1, 138
shaping 121
silver 12, 13
simultaneous engineering 40–4, 138–9
snowball technique 102
soak test 91
solder 12, 13, 127
soldering 88–9, 113
specification 64, 93–4, 139
speed restrictors 21, 22
spray painting 25
spring steel fasteners 126
sprues 11, 60, 118, 139
standardisation of components 48, 136
stock control 85–6, 90
sub-contracting 59, 80
superglues 129, 131–4
suppliers 41
surface finishing 48, 77, 78
surveys, market research 97

teamwork 8, 40–2, 51, 58–9, 90, 101
technical design 44
template 11, 139

test rigs 108
testing
    ergonomic 108
    external 103
    of PCBs 89–90, 91
    in production 51
    technical 44
thermal fabrication 127
thermal joint 127
thermoplastic 60, 62, 114–16, 139
thermoset material 114–16, 139
thermosetting adhesives 128
timber: see wood
total quality management 101
transaction authorisation 58
tube bending devices 29
Turner, Margaret 6–13
turning 120, 121

ultra-sound 62

varnish 118
veneers 75, 76, 77, 113–14
vocal challenge 72
vulcanising rubber 10–11, 139

washers 124
wasting: see machining
wax modelling 10
welding 27–8, 30, 127
Wicksteed Leisure Limited 14–15
    component assembly 32–5
    component manufacture 25–8
    design 17–19
    Discovery range 19
    jigs, fixtures and formers in 28–32
    Logworld 19, 26, 29
    Rainbow range 18
    safety 21–4
wire making 12, 136
wood 113–14
    adhesives 134
    finishes 118
    machining 120
    moisture content 26
    sawing 26, 113
    steam forming 119
wood-based products 113–14, 124–5, 129